Annuals *for* Northern California

Bob Tanem
Don Williamson

LONE PINE PUBLISHING

The Publisher: Lone Pine Publishing

10145 – 81 Avenue	1901 Raymond Avenue SW
Edmonton, AB	Suite C, Renton, WA
T6E 1W9 Canada	98055 USA

Website: http://www.lonepinepublishing.com

Canadian Cataloguing in Publication Data
Tanem, Bob.
    Annuals for northern California

    Includes index.
    ISBN 1-55105-249-0

    1. Annuals (Plants)—California. 2. Gardening—California. I. Williamson, Don, 1962– II. Title.
SB422.T36 2002   635.9'312'09794 C2001-911422-2

Editorial Director: Nancy Foulds
Project Editor: Shelagh Kubish
Editorial: Shelagh Kubish, Dawn Loewen, Denise Dykstra
Illustrations Coordinator: Carol Woo
Photo Editor: Don Williamson
Research Assistant: Laura Peters
Production Project Coordinator: Heather Markham
Book Design: Heather Markham
Cover Design: Robert Weidemann, Rod Michalchuk
Layout & Production: Heather Markham, Arlana Anderson-Hale
Image Editing: Elliot Engley, Jeff Fedorkiw, Tina Tomljenovic, Arlana Anderson-Hale
Scanning, Separations & Film: Elite Lithographers Co. Ltd.

Photography: All photographs by Tim Matheson or Tamara Eder except AA Selections 26a, 205a, 205b; © Brother Alfred Brousseau, St. Mary's College 77a; Jo-Ann Ordano/California Academy of Sciences 77b; Karen Carriere 89b; Joan de Grey 109a, 197a; Therese D'Monte 43, 144, 160, 162b; Elliot Engley 32b, 33, 34a, 34b, 35a, 35b; EuroAmerican 132, 133a, 260b; Anne Gordon 62, 63a, 63b, 64, 67b, 109b, 115b, 119a, 192, 194, 195a, 196, 228, 229b, 243a, 269b; Horticolor © 2001 Nova-Photo-Graphik/Horticolor 76, 103, 108, 198, 216c, 217a; Colin Laroque 12a; Janet Loughrey 26b, 104, 105, 193a, 193b, 195b, 197b, 229a; David McDonald 97b, 99, 102, 145b; Kim Patrick O'Leary 10, 72, 118, 123a, 133b, 153, 263a, 265b, 273a; Allison Penko 260a; Joy Spurr 60, 79b, 82, 83b, 126, 162a, 163a, 216b, 230, 244, 261b, 269a, 296a; Peter Thompstone 57b, 59b, 107a, 127a, 149a, 150b, 151b, 163b, 207b, 222, 223a, 243b, 284a, 285, 297.

Front cover photographs (clockwise from top left) sunflower, California poppy, painted daisy, Mexican sunflower, Transvaal daisy; all by Tim Matheson except painted daisy by Tamara Eder

We acknowledge the financial support of the Government of Canada through the Book Publishing Industry Development Program (BPIDP) for our publishing activities.

PC: P4

Contents

Acknowledgments

WE GRATEFULLY ACKNOWLEDGE THE FOLLOWING NURSERIES FOR THEIR cooperation: West End Nursery in San Rafael, Sunnyside Nursery in San Anselmo, Sloat Garden Center in Novato and Bayside Gardens in Belvedere. Lee and Mary Grace Bertsch allowed photographs to be taken in their garden. We thank the staff at Filoli, Elizabeth Gamble Gardens, Bonfante Gardens in Gilroy, the Leininger Community Center, Strybing Arboretum and Botanical Garden and the VanDusen Botanical Garden in Victoria, B.C. Thanks also to Kawahara Wholesale Nursery, Gaddis Nursery and Emerisa Gardens for furnishing their current plant availability lists.

The authors wish to thank Alison Beck, author of several Lone Pine gardening books, for her contributions to the text.

Bob Tanem would like to thank his customer base of 40 years, the radio station personnel and Kit Lynch, who encouraged the station to put his garden show on the air. He also thanks his wife, Bev, for her patience and sacrifices of time spent alone while he was working on this project. Most of all, he thanks the Good Lord for allowing him to retain his memory after 71 years.

Don Williamson extends thanks to his mother, Margaret Williamson, and his late father, John Williamson, for their love and support. He also thanks the team at Lone Pine Publishing, without whose help none of this would be possible. Don would also like to thank The Creator.

The Flowers at a Glance

PICTORIAL GUIDE IN ALPHABETICAL ORDER, BY COMMON NAME

African Daisy
p. 50

Ageratum
p. 52

Amaranth
p. 56

Amethyst Flower
p. 60

Angelica
p. 62

Baby's Breath
p. 64

Bachelor's Buttons
p. 68

Bacopa
p. 70

Begonia
p. 72

Bells of Ireland
p. 74

Bird's Eyes
p. 76

Black-Eyed Susan
p. 78

Black-Eyed Susan Vine
p. 82

Blanket Flower
p. 84

Blue Lace Flower
p. 86

Butterfly Weed
p. 88

California Poppy
p. 90

Candytuft
p. 94

Canterbury Bells
p. 96

Cape Marigold
p. 100

Cathedral Bells
p. 102

Chickabiddy
p. 104

China Aster
p. 106

Coreopsis
p. 114

Chinese Forget-Me-Not
p. 108

Coleus
p. 110

Corn Cockle
p. 118

Cosmos
p. 120

Creeping Zinnia
p. 124

Cup Flower
p. 126

Diascia
p. 132

Dahlia
p. 128

English Daisy
p. 134

Flowering Maple
p. 136

Forget-Me-Not
p. 144

Geranium
p. 148

Flowering Tobacco
p. 140

Fried-Egg Flower
p. 146

Globe Amaranth
p. 152

Godetia
p. 154

Impatiens
p. 160

Lobelia
p. 166

Heliotrope
p. 156

Hollyhock
p. 158

Larkspur
p. 164

Love-in-a-Mist
p. 168

Mallow
p. 174

Mexican Sunflower
p. 182

Lychnis
p. 170

Marigold
p. 178

Million Bells
p. 184

Nemesia
p. 192

Painted Daisy
p. 198

Moss Rose
p. 186

Nasturtium
p. 188

Ornamental Kale
p. 194

Painted-Tongue
p. 200

Petunia
p. 202

Phlox
p. 206

Pincushion Flower
p. 208

Poor Man's Orchid
p. 210

Pot Marigold
p. 218

Rock Cress
p. 222

Poppy
p. 214

Prickly Poppy
p. 220

Salvia
p. 224

Scarlet Runner Bean
p. 228

Snapdragon
p. 230

Spider Flower
p. 234

Statice
p. 240

Star Clusters
p. 238

Stock
p. 242

Strawflower
p. 244

Sunflower
p. 246

Sweet Potato Vine
p. 258

Swan River Daisy
p. 250

Sweet Alyssum
p. 252

Sweet Pea
p. 254

Sweet William
p. 262

Transvaal Daisy
p. 266

Vinca Rosea
p. 274

Wishbone Flower
p. 280

Verbena
p. 270

Viola
p. 276

Zinnia
p. 282

Introduction

ANNUALS ARE PLANTS THAT COMPLETE THEIR FULL LIFE CYCLE in one growing season. Within one year they germinate, mature, bloom, set seed and die. Annuals are sometimes referred to as bedding plants because they are used to provide color and fill in garden beds. Most annuals are started indoors and then transplanted into the garden after the last spring frost, but some can be sown directly in the garden. A sure sign of spring's arrival is the rush of gardeners to local garden centers, greenhouses and farmers' markets to pick out their new annuals.

Northern California's climate varies greatly depending on where you live. The following is general information for the Bay Area, the northern coast and the hot interior valleys, including the Sacramento/ Central Valley. The geography of the area is so diverse that it would be impossibe to provide more detailed climate information in this book. You should be aware of the particular conditions present in your area and garden. Keeping a journal or diary of climate conditions is a useful aid to future garden planning.

The Bay Area and coastal areas enjoy pleasant summer days with an afternoon breeze and daytime temperatures of 65–80° F. The summer fog and ocean influence keep the temperatures mild. Summer temperatures can spike from about June through September, but rarely exceed 100° F. Many annuals prefer these conditions and will provide a colorful show all summer. If you garden right on the coast, it is a good idea to select plants that can handle the constant wind and salt spray. Winters are mild on the coast with the nighttime temperatures hovering around 32° F and occasionally dropping to 23–20° F.

Summer temperatures in the interior valleys average 80–100° F from June through September and can spike to 110° F and higher. The heat will cause many annuals to stop flowering by mid- to late June. Keeping them well watered, mulched and

shaded where possible will encourage them to revive as cooler fall weather sets in. For the hot, interior valleys it is best to choose annuals that thrive in the heat. Through the short winters in the valleys, the nighttime temperatures are generally below freezing with the coldest temperatures in the 13–18° F range.

The season length does not vary greatly from the coast to the interior valleys. However, the growing season shortens dramatically in the farthest northern parts of the state, the northeastern part of the state and the higher elevations in the mountains and hillsides. The last spring frost in the Bay Area is usually around mid-March to the first part of April, and the first frost of fall is around the end of November to the early part of December. In the hot valleys the last frost in spring is around the first week in April and the first fall frost is approximately

Formal planting (above), informal (below)

the last week in November. There are areas in Northern California that rarely see frost.

The soil in Northern California usually warms up the latter part of March to the first week in April. Keep in mind, spring can start in February in many areas including the Sacramento area. If the weather is dry, most plants can be transplanted by mid-March. Transplanting any time after Easter is usually the best bet.

There is little or no rain in Northern California from the middle of March through the middle of October. Winter in the interior valleys is usually cloudy and miserable with a lot of rain. The fog can last for days or weeks. Coastal areas also receive a fair amount of rain through the winter. If it weren't for our heavy clay soils, the rain we do get would all drain away. We would be a desert and the only thing we could grow would be cactus.

Annuals are popular because they produce lots of flowers, in a wide variety of colors, over a long period of time. Many annuals bloom continuously from spring through early fall. Beyond this basic appeal, gardeners are constantly finding new ways to include annuals in their gardens, using them to accent areas in an established border, featuring them as the main attraction in a new garden, or combining them with trees, shrubs, perennials and even vegetables. Many annuals grow in a variety of conditions, from hot, dry sun to cool, damp shade. They are fun for beginners and experienced gardeners alike and because annuals are temporary and inexpensive, they can be easily replaced if they are past their prime.

There are popular annuals that many gardeners grow every year, but there are always new varieties and new species to try. Some of the most popular, easy to grow and reliable annuals include geraniums (genus *Pelargonium*), petunias, impatiens, marigolds and zinnias.

In recent years, gardeners have also developed an interest in unusual annuals. Some beautiful plants that have been overlooked in the past because they bloom later in the summer are now in wider use.

New species have been introduced from other parts of the world. There are new and sometimes improved varieties of old favorites with an expanded color range or increased pest resistance. The use of heritage varieties has been revived partly because many gardeners are concerned with over-hybridization or are interested in organic gardening. There is also the discovery that most of the older varieties have more fragrance. Many people are now enthusiastically saving seeds from and growing these heritage varieties.

The selection of annuals is increasing every year.

When new varieties are introduced, some may experience a short period of popularity but are soon forgotten. Greatly improved varieties that have been tried in gardens across the United States and Canada may be judged by members of the horticultural industry to become 'All-American Selections Winners.' These outstanding plants are dependable performers. They are most widely known, are popular and are grown by many gardeners.

Annuals in the Garden

ANNUALS ARE OFTEN USED IN combination with perennials, shrubs and trees. Because these plants bloom at different times during the growing season, including a variety of annuals in the garden provides continuous color. Annuals are also perfect for filling in bare spaces around small or leggy shrubs or between perennials that sprout late in the season. Include annuals anywhere you would like some variety and an extra splash of color—in pots staggered up porch steps or on a deck, in windowsill planters or in hanging baskets. The addition of annual flowers brightens even well-established gardens.

Annual vines can furnish a temporary screen to hide some undesirable view or an ugly part of the garden, such as compost piles, old fences, posts and sheds.

The short life of annuals allows gardeners a large degree of flexibility and freedom when planning a garden. Where trees and shrubs form the permanent structure or the bones of the garden, and perennials and groundcovers fill the spaces between them, annuals add bold patterns and bright splashes of color. Annuals give gardeners the opportunity to make the same garden look different each year. Even something as simple as a planting of impatiens under a tree can be different each year with different varieties and color combinations. When planning your garden, consult as many sources as you can. Look

through gardening books and ask friends and gardening experts for advice. Notice what you like or dislike about various gardens, and make a list of the plants you would like to include in your garden.

Informal border (above), formal border (below)

There are many styles of gardens, and annuals can be used in any of them. A symmetrical, formal garden can be enhanced by adding only a few types of annuals or by choosing annuals of all the same flower color. You may want to add a dash of the informal to the same garden by adding many different species and colors of annuals to break up the formal plantings of trees and shrubs. An informal, cottage-style garden can be a riot of plants and colors. The same garden will look less disorganized and even soothing if you use several species that bloom in cool shades of blue and purple. You can create whatever style garden you want by cleverly mixing annuals.

When choosing annuals, most people make the color, size and shape of the flowers their prime considerations. Other attributes to consider are the size and shape of the plant and leaves. Annuals grown for their foliage are attractive, particularly when used in mixed hanging baskets and planters. A variety of flower and plant sizes, shapes and colors will make your garden more interesting. Consult the Quick Reference Chart on p. 286 to help you plan.

Colors have different effects on our senses. Cool colors such as purple, blue and green are soothing and can make a small garden appear larger. Some annuals with cool colors are Lobelia, Ageratum and amethyst flowers. If you have a hectic life and need to relax when you are at home, then sitting in a garden of flowers with cool colors will help. Warm colors such as red, orange and yellow are more stimulating and appear to fill larger spaces. Warm colors can make a large, imposing garden seem warm and welcoming. Some annuals with warm colors are salvias, Pot Marigold and Mexican Sunflower.

If you work long hours and have time to enjoy your garden only in the evenings, consider pale colors such as white and yellow that show up well at dusk and even at night. Some plants have flowers that open only in the evenings and often have fragrant blossoms that add an attractive dimension to the evening garden. For example, Moonflower is a twining vine-like plant with large, white, fragrant flowers that open when the sun sets.

Foliage color varies a great deal as well. Some annuals are grown for their interesting or colorful foliage, not their flowers, and some plants have both interesting foliage and flowers. Leaves can be in any shade of green and may be covered in a soft white down or they can be so dark they appear to be almost black. Some foliage is patterned or has veins that contrast with the color of the leaves. Foliage plants such as Coleus are often used by themselves while others provide an interesting backdrop against brightly colored flowers.

Annuals with Interesting Foliage
Amaranth 'Illumination'
Coleus
Nasturtium
Sweet Potato Vine
Zonal Geranium

Coleus

Texture is another element to consider when planning a garden. Both flowers and foliage have a visual texture. Larger leaves can appear coarse in texture, and they can make a garden appear smaller and more shaded. Coarse-textured flowers appear bold and dramatic and can be seen from farther away. Small leaves appear fine in texture and create a sense of increased space and light. Fine-textured flowers appear soothing and intriguing. Sometimes the flowers and foliage of a plant have contrasting textures. Using a variety of textures helps make a garden interesting and appealing. The great thing about using annuals for

this effect is that you can change your mind and try something new next time you go to plant.

Fine-textured Annuals
Baby's Breath
Bacopa
Cup Flower
Larkspur
Lobelia
Love-in-a-mist
Swan River Daisy
Sweet Alyssum

Coarse-textured Annuals
Hollyhock
Painted Daisy
Sunflower
Sweet Potato Vine
Zinnia

Larkspur (above), 'Teddy Bear' Sunflower (below)

Getting Started

FINDING THE RIGHT ANNUALS FOR YOUR GARDEN REQUIRES experimentation and creativity. Before you start planting, consider the growing conditions in your garden; these conditions will influence not only the types of plants that you select, but also the locations in which you plant them. The plants will be healthier and less susceptible to problems if grown in optimum conditions. It is difficult to significantly modify your garden's existing conditions; an easier approach is to match the plants to the garden.

The levels of light, soil porosity and pH; the texture of soil; the amount of exposure in your garden; and the plants' tolerance to frost are guidelines for your plant selection. Sketching your garden may help you visualize the various conditions. Note shaded areas, low-lying or wet areas, exposed or windy sections, etc. Understanding your garden's growing conditions will help you learn to recognize which plants will perform best, and it can also prevent you from making costly mistakes in your planting decisions. Consult the Quick Reference Chart on p. 286.

Light

There are four levels of light in a garden: full sun, partial shade, light shade and full shade. Available light is affected by buildings, trees, fences and the position of the sun at different times of the day and year. Knowing what light is available in your garden will help you determine where to place each plant.

Plants in *full-sun* locations, such as along south-facing walls or other southern exposures, receive direct sunlight for at least six hours a day. Locations classified as *partial shade*, such as east- or west-facing walls, receive direct morning sun or late afternoon (after 4 o'clock) sun and shade for the rest of the day. *Light-shade* locations receive shade for most or all of the day, although some sunlight does filter through to ground level. An example of a light-shade location might be the ground under a small-leaved tree such as a birch. *Full-shade* locations, which would include the north side of a house, receive no direct sunlight.

Plant your annuals where they will grow best. For hot and dry areas and for low-lying, damp sections of the garden, select plants that prefer those conditions. Experimenting with annuals will help you learn about the conditions of your garden.

Sun-loving plants may become tall and straggly and flower poorly in too much shade. Shade-loving plants may get scorched leaves or even wilt and die if they get too much sun. Many plants tolerate a wide range of light conditions.

Amaranth

Marigold

Annuals for Full Sun
African Daisy
Amaranth
Bird's Eyes
Blanket Flower
Cosmos
Flowering Maple
Geranium
Heliotrope
Marigold
Moss Rose
Spider Flower
Statice

Annuals for Partial Sun or Shade
Amethyst Flower
Busy Lizzie Impatiens
Canterbury Bells
Chinese Forget-me-not
Forget-me-not
Godetia
Viola

Annuals for Sun or Shade
Begonia
Black-eyed Susan
Black-eyed Susan Vine
Canterbury Bells
Coleus
Lobelia
Morning Glory
Nasturtium
New Guinea Impatiens
Vinca Rosea

Soil
Soil quality is an extremely important element of a healthy garden. Plant roots rely on the air, water and nutrients that are held within soil. Plants also depend on soil to hold them upright. The soil in turn benefits because plant roots

Flowering Maple (full sun)

Busy Lizzie Impatiens (partial sun or shade)

Black-eyed Susan (sun or shade)

break down large soil particles. Plants prevent soil erosion by binding together small particles and reducing the amount of exposed surface. When plants die and break down, they add organic nutrients to soil and feed beneficial microorganisms.

Soil is made up of particles of different sizes. Sand particles are the largest—water drains quickly from sandy soil and nutrients tend to get washed away. Sandy soil does not compact very easily because the large particles leave air pockets between them. Clay particles, which are the smallest, can be seen only through a microscope. Clay holds the most nutrients, but it also compacts easily and has little air space. Clay is slow to absorb water and equally slow to let it drain. Most soils are composed of a combination of different particle sizes and are called loams.

Mallow

It is important to consider the pH level (the scale on which acidity or alkalinity is measured) of soil, as it influences the availability of nutrients. Most plants thrive in soil with a pH between 5.5 and 7.5. Soil pH in Northern California can be different by two or three points between the front and back yards. Testing kits can be purchased at most garden centers. There are also soil-testing labs that can fully analyze the pH as well as the quantities of various nutrients in your soil.

The acidity of soil can be reduced with the addition of horticultural lime or wood ashes. Certain wood ash such as pine and eucalyptus should not be used. The addition of elemental sulfur will lower the pH but it takes a long time for the effects to be permanent. For quicker results use aluminum sulfate or ammonium sulfate. For plants that prefer a pH that varies greatly from that of your garden soil, you might wish to use planters or create raised beds where it is easier to control and alter the pH level of soil. Always check the pH and other soil properties before you import any soil, purchased or otherwise, into your garden.

Water drainage is affected by soil type and terrain in your garden. Plants that prefer well-drained soil and do not require a large amount of moisture grow well on a sloping hillside garden with rocky soil. Water retention in these areas can be improved through the addition of organic matter. Plants that thrive on a consistent water supply or boggy conditions are ideal for low-lying areas that retain water for longer periods or hardly drain at all, such as at the base of a slope. In extremely wet areas, you can improve drainage by adding gravel and installing drainage tile. Raised beds can also be used.

Annuals for Moist Soil
Ageratum
Bacopa
Forget-me-not
Fried-egg Flower
Mallow
Spider Flower
Viola
Wishbone Flower

Annuals for Dry Soil
Butterfly Weed
Cape Marigold
Coreopsis
Cosmos
Marigold
Moss Rose
Prickly Poppy
Zinnia

Exposure
Your garden is exposed to wind, heat, cold and rain, and some plants are better adapted than others to withstand the potential damage of these forces. Buildings, walls, fences, hills, hedges, trees and even tall perennials influence and often reduce exposure.

Wind and heat are the most likely elements to cause damage to annuals. The sun can be very intense, and heat can rise quickly on a sunny afternoon. Plant annuals that tolerate or even thrive in hot weather in the hot spots in your garden. This is especially important for many parts of the Central Valley.

Fried-egg Flower

Prickly Poppy

Black-eyed Susan (above), annual containers (below)

Too much rain can be damaging to plants, as can overwatering. Early in the season, seeds or seedlings can be washed away in heavy rain. A light mulch or grow cover will help prevent this problem. Established annuals (or their flowers) can be destroyed by heavy rain. Most annuals will recover, but some, like petunias, are slow to do so. Choose plants or varieties that are quick to recover from rain damage in exposed sites. Many of the small-flowered petunia varieties recover quickly from heavy rain.

Hanging moss-lined baskets are susceptible to wind and heat exposure, losing water from the soil surface and the leaves. Water can evaporate from all sides of a moss basket, and in hot or windy locations moisture can be depleted very quickly. Hanging baskets look wonderful, but watch for wilting and water the baskets regularly to keep them looking great. I find that baskets hold up better in adverse conditions if you soak the moss or other liner in a wetting agent, such as Water In™, and add some wetting agent to the initial watering.

Frost Tolerance

When planting annuals, consider their ability to tolerate an unexpected frost. The dates for last frost and first frost vary greatly from region to region in North America. In much of Northern California, the last killing frost is usually in mid-February. In the Central Valley, it would be in mid-March, and in some of the mountainous areas the last frost is in mid-April. The map on this page gives a general idea of when you can expect your last frost date. Keep in mind that these dates can vary greatly from year to year and within the general regions. Your local garden center should be able to provide more precise information on frost expectations for your particular area.

Annuals are grouped into three categories—hardy, half-hardy or tender—based on how tolerant they are of cold weather. The Quick Reference Chart on p. 286 indicates the hardiness of all the annuals in this book to help you plan your garden.

Hardy annuals can tolerate low temperatures and even frost. They

Pot Marigold (hardy)

can be planted in the garden early and may continue to flower long into fall or even winter. I had

Average Last Spring Frost Date

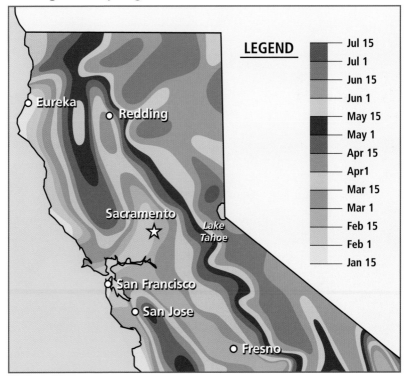

LEGEND

- Jul 15
- Jul 1
- Jun 15
- Jun 1
- May 15
- May 1
- Apr 15
- Apr1
- Mar 15
- Mar 1
- Feb 15
- Feb 1
- Jan 15

Eureka
Redding
Sacramento
Lake Tahoe
San Francisco
San Jose
Fresno

hardy *Calendula* plants close to the house, and they flowered even after a snowfall covered them. Many hardy annuals are sown directly in the garden before the last frost date.

Half-hardy annuals can tolerate a light frost but will be killed by a heavy one. These annuals can be transplanted around the last frost date and will generally benefit from being started early from seed indoors.

Tender annuals have no frost tolerance at all and might suffer even if the temperatures drop to a few degrees above freezing. These plants are often started early indoors and not planted in the garden until the last frost date has passed and the ground has had a chance to warm up. The advantage to these annuals is that they are often tolerant of hot summer temperatures.

Protecting plants from frost is relatively simple. Plants can be covered overnight with sheets, towels, burlap, row covers or even cardboard boxes. Refrain from using plastic because it doesn't retain heat and therefore doesn't provide plants with any insulation.

Petunia (half-hardy)

Scarlet Runner Bean (tender)

Preparing the Garden

TAKING THE TIME TO PROPERLY PREPARE YOUR FLOWERBEDS before you transplant will save you time and effort over summer. Many gardening problems can be avoided with good preparation and maintenance. Starting out with as few weeds as possible and with well-prepared soil that has had organic material added will give your annuals a good start. For container gardens, use potting soil because regular garden soil loses its structure when used in pots, quickly compacting into a solid mass that drains poorly.

Loosen the soil with a large garden fork and remove the weeds. Avoid working the soil when it is very wet or very dry because you will damage the soil structure by breaking down the pockets that hold air and water. Add organic matter and work it into the soil with a spade or rototiller.

Organic matter is a very important component for heavy clay soil. It increases the water-holding and nutrient-holding capacity of sandy soil and binds together the large particles. In a clay soil, organic matter will increase the soil's ability to absorb and drain water by opening up spaces between the tiny particles. Common organic additives for your soil include grass clippings, shredded leaves, peat moss, chopped straw, well-rotted manure, alfalfa pellets and compost. Alfalfa pellets supply a range of nutrients including trace elements and also contain a plant growth hormone.

Composting

Any organic matter you add will be of greater benefit to your soil if it has been composted first. Adding composted organic matter to soil adds nutrients, can adjust the pH to a more acceptable range and improves soil structure. Decaying organic matter releases acids and can help lower the soil pH. Soils with lots of organic matter are buffered from sharp rises in soil pH. If your soil is highly acidic and has lots of organic matter, it will require more amendments and time to raise the pH.

In natural environments, such as forests or meadows, compost is created when leaves, plant bits and other debris are broken down on the soil surface. This process will also take place in your garden beds if you work fresh organic matter into the soil. However, micro-organisms that break organic matter down use the same nutrients as your plants. The tougher the organic matter, the more nutrients in the soil will be used trying to break the matter down. This will rob your plants of vital nutrients, particularly nitrogen. Also, fresh organic matter and garden debris might encourage or introduce pests and diseases in your garden.

It is best to compost organic matter before adding it to your garden beds. A compost pile or bin, which can be built or purchased, creates a controlled environment where

Gardener's best friends

Plastic composters

Wooden compost bins

Materials for compost

organic matter can be fully broken down before being introduced to your garden. Good composting methods also reduce the possibility of spreading pests and diseases.

Creating compost is a simple process. Kitchen scraps, grass clippings and fall leaves will slowly break down if left in a pile. Following a few simple guidelines can speed up the process.

Your compost pile should contain both dry and fresh materials, with a larger proportion of dry matter such as chopped straw, shredded newspaper, shredded leaves or sawdust. Fresh green matter, such as vegetable scraps, grass clippings or pulled weeds, breaks down quickly and produces nitrogen, which feeds

If you use kitchen scraps, consider introducing red worms to the mix. You can have usable worm castings in as little as six weeks. The process is simple. Get a plastic container and ensure it has drainage holes. Place a light layer of shredded newspaper (avoid glossy newsprint) into the container and add all kitchen scraps, minus any meat products. You can buy red worms at any bait shop and let them eat your garbage.

Taking temperature

Finished soil

Turning compost into raised bed

the decomposer organisms while they break down the tougher dry matter.

Layer the green matter with the dry matter and mix in small amounts of soil from your garden or previously finished compost. The addition of soil or compost will introduce beneficial micro-organisms. If the pile seems very dry, sprinkle some water between the layers—the compost should be moist but not soaking wet, like a wrung-out sponge. Adding nitrogen, like that found in fertilizer, will speed up decomposition. Avoid strong concentrations of nitrogen that can kill beneficial organisms.

Each week or two, use a pitchfork to turn the pile over or poke holes into it. This will help aerate the material, which will speed up decomposition. A compost pile that is kept aerated can generate a lot of heat, reaching temperatures up to 160° F. Such a high temperature will destroy weed seeds and kill many damaging organisms. Most beneficial organisms will not be killed unless the temperature rises higher than this. To monitor the temperature of the compost near the middle of the pile you will need a thermometer that is attached to a long probe, similar to a large meat thermometer. Turn your compost once the temperature drops. Turning and aerating the pile will stimulate the process to heat up again. If you don't want to turn it, the pile can just be left to sit. It will eventually be ready to use in several months to a year.

Avoid adding diseased or pest-ridden materials to your compost pile. If the damaging organisms are not destroyed, they could be spread throughout your garden. If you do add material you suspect of harboring pests or diseases, add it near the center of the pile where the temperature is highest. Never add tomato vines from the garden.

When you can no longer recognize the matter that you put into the compost bin, and the temperature no longer rises upon turning, your compost is ready to be mixed into your garden beds. Getting to this point can take as little as one month and will leave you with organic material that is rich in nutrients and beneficial organisms.

Compost can also be purchased from most garden centers. Whether you use your own or store-bought compost, add a trowelful of compost to the planting hole and mix it into the garden soil before adding your annual.

Adding compost

Selecting Annuals

MANY GARDENERS ENJOY THE trip to the local garden center to pick out their annual plants. Other gardeners find that starting their own annuals from seed is one of the most rewarding aspects of gardening. There are benefits to both methods, and many gardeners choose to use a combination of the two. Purchasing plants is usually easier than starting plants from seeds and provides you with plants that are well grown and often already in bloom. Starting seeds can be impractical. The process requires space and facilities, and some seeds require specific conditions that are difficult to achieve in a house or they have erratic germination rates. Starting from seed may offer you a greater selection of species and varieties, as seed catalogs often list many more plants than are offered at garden centers. Starting annuals from seed is discussed on p. 33.

Purchased annual plants are grown in a variety of containers. Some are sold in individual pots, some in divided cell-packs and others in undivided trays. Each type has advantages and disadvantages.

Annuals in individual pots are usually well established and have plenty of space for root growth. These annuals have probably been seeded in flat trays and then transplanted into individual pots once they developed a few leaves. The cost of labor, pots and soil can make this option somewhat more expensive. If you are planting a large area you may also find it difficult to transport large numbers of plants of this size.

Annuals grown in cell-packs are often inexpensive and hold several plants, making them easy to transport. There is less damage to the roots of the plants when they are transplanted, but because each cell is quite small, it doesn't take too long for a plant to become root-bound.

Annuals grown in undivided trays have plenty of room for root growth and can be left in the trays for longer than other types of containers; however, their roots tend to become entangled, making the plants difficult to separate.

Regardless of the type of container, often the best plants to choose are those not yet flowering. These plants are younger and are unlikely to be root-bound. Check for roots emerging from the holes at the

Lobelia grown in cell packs

Plant on left is root-bound.

bottom of the cells or gently remove the plant from the container to look at the roots. Too many roots mean that the plant is too mature for the container, especially if the roots are wrapped around the inside of the container in a thick web. Such plants are slow to establish once they are transplanted into the garden.

The plants should be compact and have good color. Healthy leaves look firm and vibrant. Unhealthy leaves may be wilted, chewed or discolored. Tall, leggy plants have likely been deprived of light. Sickly plants may not survive being transplanted and may spread pests or diseases to the rest of your garden.

Once you get your annuals home, water them if they are dry. Annuals growing in small containers may require water more than once a day. Begin to harden off the plants so they can be transplanted into the garden as soon as possible. Your annuals are probably accustomed to growing in the sheltered environment of a greenhouse, and they will need to become accustomed to the climate outdoors. They can be placed outdoors in a lightly shaded spot each day and brought into a sheltered porch, garage or house at night for about a week. This will acclimatize them to your environment. Many nurseries grow their plants in the same exposure where they would be grown in the garden and hardening off may be unnecessary. It is a good idea to ask where your potential new annuals have been grown. If you are unsure follow the above guidelines.

Starting Annuals from Seed

STARTING ANNUALS FROM SEED can be fun and will provide you with a wider variety of plants than those available at a garden center. There are dozens of catalogs from different growers offering a varied selection of annuals that you can start from seed.

Starting your own annuals can save you money, particularly if you have a large area to plant. The necessary basic equipment is not expensive, and most seeds can be started in a sunny window. You may, however, encounter a problem of limited space. One or two trays of annuals don't take up too much room, but storing more than that may be unreasonable. This is why many gardeners start a few specialty plants themselves but purchase the bulk of their annuals already started from a garden center.

Each plant in this book will have specific information on starting it from seed, but there are a few basic steps that can be followed for all seeds. The easiest way for the home gardener to start seeds is in cell-packs in trays with plastic dome covers. The cell-packs keep roots separated, and the tray and dome keep moisture in.

Seeds can also be started in pots, peat pots or peat pellets. The advantage to starting in peat pots or pellets is that you will not disturb the roots when you transplant your annuals. When planting peat pots into the garden, be sure to remove the top couple of inches of pot. If any of the pot is sticking up out of the soil, it can wick moisture away from your plant. It is

Annual · Annuelle   Annual · Annuelle

also advisable to slice vertically down each side of the peat pot or peat pellet. This ensures the roots will be able to grow out past the pot and into the soil. Another seeding method that does not disturb roots is starting the seed in a 4" pot. When it is time to plant, place the 4" pot in the ground and backfill around the pot. Lift the pot out of the ground and gently remove the plant and rootball from the pot. Gently set the plant into the pre-shaped hole, and water to settle the soil around the rootball. This method works very well as long as the plants are not root-bound.

Use a growing mix (soil mix) that is intended for seedlings. These mixes are very fine, usually made from peat moss, vermiculite and perlite. The mix will have good water-holding capacity and will have been sterilized to prevent pests and diseases from attacking the seedlings. Using sterile soil mix, keeping soil evenly moist and maintaining good air circulation will prevent the problem of damping off. It is heartbreaking to see the tiny plants you have watched sprout from seeds flop over and die from damping off. Damping off is caused by a variety of soil-borne fungi, and the affected seedling will appear to have been pinched at soil level. The pinched area blackens, and the seedling topples over and dies. Damping off can be reduced or prevented by spreading a 1/4" layer of peat moss over the seedbed.

Fill your pots, cell packs or seed trays with the soil mix and firm it down slightly. Soil that is too firmly packed will not drain well. Wet the soil before planting your seeds to prevent them from getting washed around. Large seeds can be planted one or two to a cell, but smaller seeds

may have to be placed in a folded piece of paper and sprinkled evenly over the soil surface. Very tiny seeds, like those of Begonia, can be mixed with fine sand before being sprinkled evenly across the soil surface. After sowing the tiny seeds and sand, transplant when the first true leaves appear, as that is when the plants will be big enough to handle.

Small seeds will not need to be covered with any more soil, but medium-sized seeds can be lightly covered, and large seeds can be poked into the soil. Some seeds need to be exposed to light in order to germinate; these should be left on the soil surface regardless of their size.

Place pots or flats of seeds in clear plastic bags to retain humidity while the seeds are germinating. Many planting trays come with clear plastic covers, which can be placed over the trays to keep the moisture in. Remove the plastic once the seeds have germinated. You should check the progress of your seedlings daily.

A cold frame is a wonderful tool. It can be used to protect tender plants over winter, to start seeds early in winter and spring, to harden plants off before moving them to the garden, to protect fall-germinating seedlings and young cuttings and to

Seeding into cell packs

Seeding very small seeds

start seeds that need a cold treatment if your area gets cold enough. This mini-greenhouse structure is built so that ground level on the inside of the cold frame is lower than on the outside. The angled, hinged lid is fitted with glass. The soil around the outside of the cold frame insulates the plants inside. The lid lets light in and collects some heat during the day and prevents rain from damaging tender plants. If the interior gets too hot, the lid can be raised to create ventilation.

Water seeds and small seedlings with a fine spray from a hand-held mister—small seeds can easily be washed around if the spray is too strong. I recall working at a greenhouse where the seed trays containing Sweet Alyssum were once watered a little too vigorously. Sweet Alyssum was soon found growing just about everywhere—with other plants, in the gravel on the floor, even in some of the flowerbeds. The lesson is 'water gently.' A less hardy species would not have come up at all if its seeds were washed into an adverse location. The amount and timing of watering is critical to successful growing from seed. Most germinated seed and young seedlings will perish if the soil is allowed to dry out. Strive

to maintain a consistently moist soil, which may mean watering lightly 2–3 times a day. As the seedlings get bigger you can cut back on the number of times you have to water but you will have to water a little heavier. A rule of thumb is when the seedlings have their first true leaves you can cut back to watering once a day.

Small seedlings will not need to be fertilized until they have about four or five true leaves. Seeds provide all the energy and nutrients that young seedlings require. Fertilizer will cause the plants to have soft growth that is more susceptible to insects and diseases, and too strong a fertilizer can burn tender young roots. When the first leaves that sprouted begin to shrivel, the plant has used up all its seed energy and you can begin to use a fertilizer diluted to one-quarter strength when feeding seedlings or young plants.

If the seedlings get too big for their containers before you are ready to plant in your garden, you may have to transplant the seedlings to larger pots to prevent them from becoming root-bound. Harden plants off by exposing them to sunnier, windier conditions and fluctuating outdoor temperatures for increasing periods of time every day for at least a week.

Potting seedlings

Potted nasturtium seedlings

Some seeds can be started directly in the garden. The procedure is similar to that of starting seeds indoors. Start with a well-prepared bed that has been smoothly raked. The small furrows left by the rake will help hold moisture and prevent the seeds from being washed away. Sprinkle the seeds onto the soil and cover them lightly with peat moss or more soil. Larger seeds can be planted slightly deeper into the soil. You may not want to sow very tiny seeds directly in the garden because they can blow or wash away. The soil should be kept moist to ensure even germination. Use a gentle spray to avoid washing the seeds around the bed because they inevitably pool into dense clumps. Covering your newly seeded bed with chicken wire, an old sheet or some thorny branches will discourage pets from digging. Covering the seeded area with a row cover also discourages pets and helps speed up germination. Remove the cover once the seeds have germinated.

Some annuals are better choices than others for direct sowing in the garden. Annuals that are difficult to transplant or that have large or quick-germinating seeds are good to direct sow.

Annuals for Direct Seeding

Amaranth
Baby's Breath
Bachelor's Buttons
Bird's Eyes
Black-eyed Susan
Blue Lace Flower
California Poppy
Candytuft
Cosmos
Forget-me-not
Fried-egg Flower
Godetia
Larkspur
Lychnis
Mallow
Nasturtium
Painted Daisy
Phlox
Poppy
Pot Marigold
Scarlet Runner Bean
Spider Flower
Sunflower
Sweet Alyssum
Sweet Pea
Zinnia

California Poppy

Nasturtium with Sweet Alyssum

Growing Annuals

ONCE YOUR ANNUALS ARE HARDENED OFF THEY ARE READY TO be transplanted. If your beds are prepared, you can start. The only tool you are likely to need is a trowel. Be sure you have set aside enough time to do the job. You don't want to have young plants out of their pots and not finish planting them. If they are left out in the sun they can quickly dry out and die. To help avoid this problem, choose an overcast day for planting. Early mornings or evenings are also good times to plant.

Planting

Moisten the soil to aid the removal of the plants from their containers. Push on the bottom of the cell or pot with your thumb to ease the plants out. If the plants were growing in an undivided tray then you will have to gently untangle the roots. If the roots are very tangled, immerse them in water and wash some of the soil away. This should free the plants from one another. If you must handle the plant, hold it by a leaf to avoid crushing the stems. Remove and discard any damaged leaves or growth.

The rootball should contain a network of white plant roots. If the rootball is densely matted and twisted, otherwise known as root-bound, score the rootball vertically on four sides with a sharp knife or gently break it apart in order to encourage the roots to extend and grow outward. New root growth will start from the cuts or breaks, allowing the plant to spread outwards.

Insert your trowel into the soil and pull it towards you, creating a wedge. Place your annual into the hole and firm the soil around the plant with your hands. Water newly planted annuals gently but thoroughly. They will need regular watering for a couple of weeks until they become established.

You don't have to be conservative when arranging your flowerbeds. There are more design choices than simple straight rows, though formal bedding-out patterns are still used in many parks and formal gardens. Today's plantings are often made in casual groups and natural drifts. The quickest way to space out your annuals is to remove them from their containers and randomly place them onto the bed. You will get a nice mix of colors and plants without too much planning. Plant a small section at a time so that the roots don't dry out. This is especially important if you have a large bed to plant.

If you are just adding a few annuals here and there to accent your shrub and perennial plantings, then plant in groups. Random clusters of three to five plants add color and interest to your garden. Always plant groups of the same plants in odd numbers for a more natural effect.

Combine the low-growing or spreading annuals with tall or bushy ones. Keep the tallest plants towards the back and smallest plants towards the front of the bed. This improves the visibility of the plants and hides the often-unattractive lower limbs of taller plants. Be sure also to leave your plants enough room to spread. They may look lonely and far apart when you first plant them, but annuals will quickly grow to fill in the space you leave.

There are no strict rules when it comes to planting and spacing. We suggest spacing distances in each plant account. A good rule of thumb for spacing annuals is to space slightly less than the plant's spread. This gives a good, full effect when the plants mature. Some plants need more space in between to encourage good air circulation. This is also noted in the plant accounts. Plant your annuals the way you like them, whether it is in straight rows or in a jumble of colors, shapes and sizes. The idea is to have fun and to create something that you will enjoy once your garden is planted.

Some annuals require more care than others do, but most require minimal care once established.

I once asked an internationally known Japanese landscaper what he did to arrange his plants. 'I do three rock,' he told me. 'Three rock?' I asked. 'I'll show you.' He turned his back on the landscape and tossed three shiny rocks behind him. He then instructed the laborers to put the plants where the rocks landed. Maybe this wasn't too scientific, but he was getting paid very well for it. I've been a three and five rock person ever since.

Ongoing maintenance will keep your garden looking its best. Weeding, watering and deadheading are a few of the basic tasks that when performed regularly can save you a big job later on.

Weeding

Controlling weed populations keeps the garden healthy and neat. Weeding may not be anyone's favorite task, but it is essential. Weeds compete with your plants for light, nutrients and space, and they can also harbor pests and diseases.

Weeds can be pulled by hand or with a hoe. Shortly after a rainfall, when the soil is soft and damp, is the easiest time to pull weeds. A hoe scuffed quickly across the soil surface will uproot small weeds and sever larger ones from their roots. Try to pull weeds out while they are still small. Once they are large enough to flower, many will quickly set seed; then you will have an entire new generation to worry about.

Mulching

A layer of mulch around your plants will prevent weeds from germinating by preventing sufficient light from reaching the seeds. Those that do germinate will be smothered or will find it difficult to get to the soil surface, exhausting their energy before getting a chance to grow. Weeds are very easy to pull from a mulched bed.

Mulch also helps maintain consistent soil temperatures and ensures that moisture is retained more effectively, which means you will not need to water as much. In areas that

receive heavy wind or rainfall, mulch can protect soil and prevent erosion. Mulching is effective in garden beds and planters especially where summer temperatures can climb over 100° F.

Organic mulches include materials such as compost, bark chips, grass clippings or shredded leaves. These mulches add nutrients to soil as they break down, thus improving the quality of the soil and ultimately the health of your plants. Shredded newspaper also makes wonderful mulch. Use only newsprint and not glossy paper. Shredded cedar bark or redwood bark has an added bonus of a naturally occurring fungicide, which can help prevent root rot.

Spread a couple of inches of mulch over the soil after you have planted your annuals. Don't pile the mulch too thick in the area immediately around the crowns and stems

Weeds and tools

Mulched garden

of your annuals. Mulch that is too close up against plants traps moisture, prevents air circulation and encourages fungal disease. As your mulch breaks down over summer, be sure to replenish it.

Watering

Water thoroughly but infrequently when plants are established. Annuals given a light sprinkle of water every day will develop roots that stay close to the soil surface, making the plants vulnerable to heat and dry spells. Annuals given a deep watering once a week will develop a deeper root system. In a dry spell they will be adapted to seeking out the water trapped deeper in the ground. Use mulch to prevent water from evaporating out of the soil. We advise that you do the majority of your watering in the morning. This approach allows any moisture on the plant to dry during the day, thereby lessening the chances of developing fungal disease.

To avoid overwatering, check the amount of moisture in the rootzone before applying any water. Feel the surface or poke your finger into the top 1–2" of soil. You can also try rolling a bit of the soil from around the plant into a ball. Soil that forms a ball is moist and needs no extra water.

Be sure the water penetrates at least 4" into the soil. To save time, money and water you may wish to install an irrigation system. Irrigation systems apply the water exactly where it is needed, near the roots, and reduce the amount of water lost to evaporation. They can be very complex or very simple, depending on your needs. A simple irrigation system would involve laying soaker hoses around your garden beds under the mulch. Consult with your local garden centers or landscape professionals for more information.

Annuals in hanging baskets and planters will probably need to be watered more frequently than plants growing in the ground. The smaller the container the more often the plants will need watering. Containers and hanging moss baskets may need to be watered twice daily during hot, sunny weather. If the soil in your container dries out, you will have to water several times to make sure water is absorbed throughout the planting medium. Dig into the soil, and if it is dry at all, water more. There are products on the market that can help water penetrate into dry soils, such as Water-In™. These products are often added to peat moss and soil mixes to improve their water-holding abilities.

Fertilizing

Your local garden center should carry a good supply of both organic and chemical fertilizers. Follow the directions carefully because using too much fertilizer can kill your plants by burning their roots. Whenever possible, use organic fertilizers because they are generally less concentrated and less likely to burn your plants.

Many annuals will flower most profusely if they are fertilized regularly. Some gardeners fertilize hanging baskets and container gardens every time they water—use a very dilute fertilizer so as not to burn the plants. However, too much fertilizer can result in plants that produce weak growth that is susceptible to pest and disease problems. Some plants, such as nasturtiums, grow better without fertilizer and may produce few or no flowers when fertilized excessively.

Fertilizer comes in many forms. Liquids or water-soluble powders are easiest to use when watering. Slow-release pellets or granules are mixed into the garden or potting soil or sprinkled around the plant and left to work over summer.

Here are some of my favorite fertilizers. VF 11™ is a liquid that can be added to every watering. It can also be sprayed on the foliage on a weekly basis. Don't worry that the fertilizer concentration is so light. I have found that less is better. Formulas that contain large amounts of chemicals are a waste because the plant can't use them right away. Chicken manure is better than other animal fertilizers for working into the soil. Alfalfa pellets contain triacontanol, which is a very powerful plant growth hormone. It stimulates the roots of plants so that they actually use the fertilizer you give them. Bone meal is touted as a wonderful fertilizer for bulbs. Unfortunately it attracts animals to the planted location and can cause major destruction. Fish emulsion is great to use as a liquid. I apply it at one-third the recommended rate. This way you can use it more often without the danger of burning the plant.

Grooming

Good grooming will keep your annuals healthy and neat, make them flower more profusely and help prevent pest and disease problems. Grooming may include pinching, deadheading, trimming and staking.

Pinch out any straggly growth and the tips of leggy annuals. Plants in cell-packs may have developed tall and straggly growth in an attempt to get light. Pinch back the long growth when transplanting to encourage bushier growth. Take off any yellow or dying leaves.

Deadheading flowers is an important step in maintaining the health of annuals. To save yourself a big job later, get into the habit of picking off spent flowers as you are looking around your garden. Some plants, such as impatiens and begonias, are self-grooming, meaning that they drop their faded blossoms on their own. Others perform much better if you deadhead them regularly.

If annuals appear tired and withered by mid-summer, try trimming them back to encourage a second blooming. Mounding or low-growing annuals, such as petunias, respond well to trimming. Take your garden shears and trim back a quarter or half of the plant growth. New growth will sprout along with a second flush of flowers. It is a good idea to give them a light fertilizing at this time.

Some annuals have very tall growth and cannot be pinched or trimmed. Instead, remove the main shoot after it blooms and side shoots may develop. Tall annuals, such as Larkspur, require staking with bamboo or other tall, thin stakes. Tie the plant loosely to the stake—strips of nylon hosiery make soft ties that won't cut into the plant. Make sure the strips are narrow so as not to show. Stake bushy plants with twiggy branches or tomato cages. Insert the twigs or cages around the plant when it is small and it will grow to fill in and hide the stakes.

Impatiens plants are self-cleaning

Marigolds need deadheading

Annuals from Perennials

MANY OF THE PLANTS GROWN as annuals are actually perennials, such as geraniums (*Pelargonium*), that originate in warmer climates and are unable to survive cooler winters. Other plants grown as annuals are biennials, such as forget-me-nots, which are started very early in the year to allow them to grow and flower in a single season. These perennials and biennials are listed as such in the species accounts. There are several techniques you can use in order to keep these plants for more than one summer.

Perennials with tuberous roots can be stored over winter and re-planted in late winter or early spring. Plants such as dahlias can be dug up in fall after the plant dies back. If there is the chance the ground may freeze, dig up the tubers prior to the ground freezing. Shake the loose dirt away from the roots and let them dry out a bit in a cool dark place. Once they are dry, the rest of the soil should brush away. Dust the tubers with an anti-fungal powder, such as garden sulfur (found at garden centers), before storing them in moist peat moss or coarse sawdust. Keep them in a cool, dark, dry place that doesn't freeze. Pot them if they start to sprout and keep them in a bright window and in moist soil. They should be potted by late winter or early spring so they will be ready for spring planting.

Cuttings can be taken from large or fast-growing plants such as Black-eyed Susan Vine and grown over winter for new spring plants.

If this sounds like too much work, replace plants each year and leave the hard work to the growers.

If you like the foliage of a seed-grown plant, such as Coleus, you can preserve the plants over the winter. Take 3" long tip cuttings in fall as the weather cools. Remove all leaves except those at the tip. Place them in water or moist planting mix until they root. Keep cuttings out of the sun until rooted, which should be about six weeks. Place the rooted cuttings in a sunny window until the middle of March. Introduce the plants slowly to the outside. Leave them outside in shade during the day and bring them inside at night. In about two weeks they can be transplanted to their summer home.

Problems & Pests

NEW ANNUALS ARE PLANTED EACH YEAR, AND MANY GARDENERS grow different species every year. These factors make it difficult for pests and diseases to find their preferred host plants and establish a population. It is a good idea to confuse insects and prevent diseases by planting different varieties of annuals each year instead of using the same varieties in the same beds year after year. However, because annual species are often grown together in masses, any problems that set in are likely to attack many of the plants.

For many years pest control meant spraying or dusting, with the goal of eliminating every pest in the landscape. A more moderate approach advocated today is known as IPM (Integrated Pest Management or Integrated Plant Management). The goal of IPM is to reduce pest problems to levels at which only negligible damage is done. Of course, you, the gardener, must determine what degree of damage is acceptable to you. Consider whether a pest's damage is localized or covers the entire plant. Will the damage being done kill the plant or is it only affecting the outward appearance? Are there methods of controlling the pest without chemicals?

Chemicals are the last resort, because they may do more harm than good. They can endanger the gardener and his or her family and pets, and they kill as many good as bad organisms, leaving the whole garden vulnerable to even worse attacks. A good IPM program includes learning about your plants and the conditions they need for healthy growth, what pests might affect your plants, where and when to look for those pests and

Frogs eat many insect pests.

how to control them. Keep records of pest damage because your observations can reveal patterns useful in spotting recurring problems and in planning your maintenance regime.

There are four steps in effective and responsible pest management. Cultural controls are the most important. Physical controls should be attempted next, followed by biological controls. Resort to chemical controls only when the first three possibilities have been exhausted.

Cultural controls are the gardening techniques you use in the day-to-day care of your garden. Keeping your plants as healthy as possible is the best defense against pests. Growing annuals in the conditions they prefer and keeping your soil healthy, with plenty of organic matter, are just two of the cultural controls you can use to keep pests manageable. Choose resistant varieties of annuals that are not prone to problems. Space the plants so that they have good air circulation around them and are not stressed from competing for light, nutrients and space. Remove plants from the landscape if the same pests decimate them every year. A good example of this is the budworm, which attacks petunias, snapdragons and geranium (*Pelargonium*) plants. If you have had problems with budworms, plant zinnias or other annuals that are not attacked. Remove and either burn or take to a permitted dump site diseased foliage and branches, and prevent the spread of disease by keeping your gardening tools clean and by tidying up fallen leaves and dead plant matter at the end of every growing season.

My favorite method of treating infected material is to place it into a black plastic bag and leave it in the hot sun for a week. The high heat kills micro-organisms that would be dangerous. I then put it into the garbage that will be picked up and hauled away.

Compost Tea
Mix 1 to 2 pounds of compost
in 5 gallons of water. Let sit
for 4–7 days. For use, dilute
the mix until it resembles
weak tea. Apply as a foliar
spray or use during normal
watering.

Physical controls are generally used to combat insect problems. An example of such a control is picking insects off plants by hand, which is not as daunting as it may seem if you catch the problem when it is just beginning. Large, slow insects are particularly easy to pick off. A small, hand-held vacuum cleaner can be used for smaller pests such as whiteflies. Other physical controls include barriers that stop insects from getting to the plant and traps that catch or confuse insects. Physical control of diseases often necessitates removing the infected plant part or parts to prevent the spread of the problem.

Biological controls make use of populations of predators that prey on pests. Animals such as birds, snakes, frogs, spiders, lady beetles and certain bacteria can play an important role in keeping pest populations at a manageable level. Encourage these creatures to take up permanent residence in your garden. A birdbath and birdfeeder will encourage birds to enjoy your yard and feed on a wide variety of insect pests. Many beneficial insects are probably already living in your landscape, and you can encourage them to stay by planting appropriate food sources. Many beneficial insects eat nectar from flowers such as the perennial yarrow.

Chemical controls should rarely be necessary, but if you must use them there are some 'organic' options available. Organic sprays are no less dangerous than chemical ones, but they will break down into harmless compounds. The main drawback to using any chemicals is that they may also kill the beneficial insects you have been trying to attract to your garden. Organic chemicals are available at most garden centers. Follow the manufacturer's instructions carefully. A large amount of insecticide is not going to be any more effective in controlling pests than the recommended amount. Note that if a particular pest is not listed on the package, that product will not control it. Proper and early identification of pests is vital to finding a quick solution.

Whereas cultural, physical, biological and chemical controls are all possible defenses against insects, diseases can only be controlled culturally. It is most often weakened plants that succumb to diseases. Healthy plants can often fight off illness, although some diseases can infect plants regardless of their level of health. Prevention is often the only hope: once a plant has been infected, it should probably be destroyed to prevent the disease from spreading.

Rule of thumb for mixing horticultural oil: 5 tablespoons oil per 1 gallon of water.

Coffee Grounds Spray
Boil 2 pounds used coffee grounds in 3 gallons water for about 10 minutes. Allow to cool; strain the grounds out of the mixture. Apply as a spray.

About this Guide

THE ANNUALS IN THIS BOOK ARE ORGANIZED ALPHABETICALLY by their local common names. Additional common names and Latin names appear after the primary reference. Quick identification information on height, spread and flower color are the first details given on each plant. The **Quick Reference Chart** at the back of the book will be a handy guide to planning diversity in your garden.

For each entry, we describe our favorite recommended or alternate species, but keep in mind that many more hybrids, cultivars and varieties are often available. Check with your local greenhouses or garden centers when making your selection. The **Flowers at a Glance** section shows one flower from each entry so you can become familiar with the different flowers.

Pests or diseases common to a plant, if any, are listed for each entry.

The section 'Problems & Pests' in the Introduction and the Glossary of Pests & Diseases at the back of the book provide information on identifying and solving the common problems that can plague plants in your garden.

Because our region is so climatically diverse, we refer to the seasons in only the general sense. The last frost date is specific to your area; refer to the map on p. 25 and consult your local garden center.

THE
ANNUALS

FOR NORTHERN CALIFORNIA

African Daisy
Monarch of the Veldt
Arctotis (Venidium)

Height: 12–24" **Spread:** 12–16" **Flower color:** pink, orange, yellow, red, white

AFRICAN DAISIES are great choices for the cooler areas of the Bay Area where their repeat blooming will ensure wonderful color. In the hot interior areas they'll bloom in spring and again in fall until first frost. They combine well with such annuals as *Salvia* 'Red Hot Sally' or 'Victoria' and Dusty Miller.

Planting

Seeding: Indoors in early spring; direct sow after last frost

Transplanting: Mid-March through May; in fall in milder climates

Spacing: 12–16"

Growing

Choose a location in **full sun**. The soil should be **average, moist** and **well drained**. African daisies don't mind sandy soil and tolerate heavy clay soil. They also tolerate drought well, particularly if the weather isn't too hot. Although African daisies are considered annuals in many areas, in the Bay Area the plants can over-winter. It is a good idea if you live in a frost-free area to mulch the plants in the fall to protect the plants. They are at their flowering best if treated as annuals.

Seeds started indoors should be planted in peat pots or peat pellets to avoid disturbing the roots when the seedlings are transplanted outdoors. Plants with disturbed or damaged roots take longer to become established, and a plant may not recover at all if the damage is excessive. The seeds of African daisies do not keep, so new seeds should be purchased or collected each year.

Deadheading prolongs the blooming season long into fall.

Tips

African daisies can be grouped or massed in beds, borders and cutting gardens. They do quite well grown in planters and other containers.

African daisies make a good addition to a deer-resistant garden.

Recommended

Several hybrids bear striking flowers. **Harlequin Hybrids** grow up to 20" tall and spread 12" wide. They do not come true to type from seed and are propagated by cuttings. Flowers may be pink, red, white, orange or yellow.

A. fastuosa (Monarch of the Veldt, Cape Daisy) has bright orange flowers with a purple spot at the base of each petal. It grows 12–24" tall and spreads 12". **'Orange Prince'** grows 24" tall and has golden orange flowers with a dark purple, almost black, center. Keep the plant spacing tight for the best show. **'Zulu Prince'** bears large creamy white or yellow flowers with bands of brown and orange at the base of each petal.

A. stoechadifolia var. *grandis* (African Daisy) has 3" wide blooms that are white with a yellow ring, and the undersides of the petals are pale lavender blue. The plant has a nice bushy form and grows 24" tall and 16" wide.

Problems & Pests

African daisies do poorly in cold, wet weather. Watch for aphids, leaf miners, downy mildew and leaf spot.

Ageratum
Floss Flower
Ageratum

Height: 6–30" **Spread:** 6–12" **Flower color:** white, pink, mauve, blue

WITH THE MAGIC of hybridization this wonderful, colorful plant has become a mainstay in many gardens throughout Northern California. My first impression of this plant over 30 years ago did not inspire me. I found it somewhat useful when blue flowers were called for, but it needed cutting back constantly and grew very sparsely. The newer hybrids require very little grooming. I have had a lot of fun combining Ageratum with the shorter white impatiens.

Planting

Seeding: Indoors in early spring; direct sow after last frost

Transplanting: Once soil has warmed

Spacing: 4–12"

Growing

Ageratum prefers **full sun,** but it will tolerate partial shade. The soil should be **fertile, moist** and **well drained.** Using a great deal of compost or planting mix will aid in Ageratum's growth and blooming.

Don't cover the seeds; they need light to germinate.

Ageratum doesn't like dried-out soil, so it is a good candidate for a moisture-retaining mulch, which will cut down on watering. Don't mulch too thickly or too close to the base of the plant, or the plant may develop crown rot or root rot.

'Blue Hawaii' (this page)

Ageratum is a genus comprising about 40 species of annuals, perennials and shrubs. Naturalized in many areas, these species occupy diverse habitats from tropical South America to warm-temperate North America.

Tips

The smaller varieties, which become almost completely covered with the fluffy flowerheads, make excellent edging plants. They are also attractive grouped in masses or grown in planters. The taller varieties are useful in the center of a flowerbed and make interesting cut flowers. Ageratum works well in hanging moss baskets when combined with white impatiens, yellow violas and Sweet Alyssum.

The original species was a tall, leggy plant that was not considered attractive enough for the annual border but was often relegated to the cutting garden. New cultivars are much more compact, and Ageratum is now a proudly displayed annual.

Cutting back old and dying blooms after the first flush of color in mid-spring will increase blooms at a later date.

The genus name Ageratum *is derived from the Greek and means 'without age,' a reference to the long-lasting flowers.*

Recommended

A. houstonianum forms a large, leggy mound that can grow up to 24" tall. Clusters of fuzzy blue, white or pink flowers are held above the foliage. Many cultivars are available; most have been developed to maintain a low, compact form that is more useful in the border. **'Bavaria'** grows about 10" tall with blue and white bicolored flowers. **'Blue Hawaii'** is a compact, 6–8" tall plant with blue flowers. **'Blue Horizon'** has 3" wide clusters of blue flowers that bloom from early summer to frost. The plant has very uniform growth and reaches a height of 24–30". **'Blue Puffs'** ('Blue Danube') grows uniformly to 6–8" tall and 9–12" wide. It bears lavender blue or pink flowers. **'Pink Powderpuffs'** is a compact plant 9" tall and 9–12" wide, with pink flowers. **'Red Top'** has bright pink to red blooms and grows 24–30" tall. **'Summer Snow'** has white flowers.

Problems & Pests

Plant Ageratum in a location with good air circulation to help prevent powdery mildew and other fungal problems.

Ageratum blooms can be cut, bundled together with rubber bands and hung upside down in a location with good air circulation. Use the dried flowers in floral arrangements.

'Pink Powderpuffs' (above)

Amaranth
Love-lies-bleeding
Amaranthus

Height: 3–6' **Spread:** 12–30"
Flower color: red, yellow or green;
flowers inconspicuous in some species

I WAS FIRST INTRODUCED to Amaranth as Chinese Spinach. It was cooked and served as a wonderful vegetable. Health food stores have Amaranth flour and bulk Amaranth seeds, which have excellent food value. Joseph's Coat, with its colorful foliage that looks like Poinsettia, can add a beautiful accent to any sunny location.

Planting

Seeding: Indoors about three weeks before last frost; direct sow once soil has warmed to at least 70° F

Transplanting: After last frost

Spacing: 12–24"

Several species of Amaranthus *are used as potherbs and vegetables because the leaves are high in protein; other species are grown as grain crops.*

Growing

A location in **full sun** is preferable. The soil should be **poor to average** and **well drained**. Seeds started indoors should be planted in peat pots or pellets to avoid disturbing the roots when transplanting them.

Tips

Love-lies-bleeding and Purple Amaranth are attractive grouped in tall borders, where they require little care or water over summer. Joseph's Coat is a bright and striking plant that is best used as an annual specimen plant rather than in a grouping, where it can quickly become overwhelming. It is also attractive when mixed with large foliage plants in the back of a border.

Planting in rich soil or overfertilizing these plants will result in tall, soft, weak stems prone to falling over. Joseph's Coat loses some of its leaf color when overfertilized; its colors will be more brilliant in poorer soil. Love-lies-bleeding has

A. caudatus

Amaranth can be used dried or fresh for floral arrangements and craft projects.

A. tricolor

the habit of self-sowing year after year. Unwanted plants are easy to uproot when they are young.

It is best to use a slow-release organic fertilizer such as alfalfa pellets or compost when growing any amaranth.

Recommended

A. caudatus (Love-lies-bleeding) has erect stems that support fluffy and long red, yellow or green drooping flowers that can be air dried. It grows 36–60" tall and 18–30" wide. **'Green Thumb'** bears upright spikes of green flowers. **'Pony Tails'** has large, raspberry red flowers in long, thick, drooping clusters resembling a knotted rope. Flowering is best around mid-summer. The flower clusters are sturdy enough to grab onto or squeeze without damaging them. **'Viridis'** bears bright green flowers that fade to cream-green as they mature.

A. paniculatus *(A. cruentus)* (Purple Amaranth, Red Amaranth, Prince's Feather) is a tall, erect plant reaching a height of 5' and spreading 18–24". Spikes of red or purple flowers are produced from summer to early fall. **'Hot Biscuits'**

'Viridis'

'Hot Biscuits'

has chestnut brown flowers that bloom from early to late summer, fading to golden brown with age.

A. tricolor (Joseph's Coat) is a bushy, upright plant with brightly colored foliage. It grows up to 5' tall and spreads 12–24". The variegated foliage can be green, red, bronze, chocolaty purple, orange, yellow or gold. '**Illumination**' has hanging foliage in crimson and gold and inconspicuous flowers. It grows 4' tall and 12" wide.

Problems & Pests

Cold nights below 50° F will cause leaf drop. Rust, leaf spot, root rot, aphids and some viral diseases are potential problems. Leaf miners are the biggest problem.

Amaranthus *means 'not fading,' a reference to the plants' tendency to retain flower or leaf color.*

A. paniculatus

'Illumination'

'Green Thumb'

Amethyst Flower
Browallia

Height: 8–24" **Spread:** 8–24"
Flower color: violet, blue, white

WHEN I FIRST CARRIED amethyst flower plants in my nurseries, I didn't have much luck with them. I kept them in the shade and watered them a lot. When I put them in the sun for part of the day and changed the soil to a well-drained soil mix, they were really something. They are now one of my favorites. The dark green foliage and wonderful blooms are outstanding on their own, and the plants make an interesting, eye-catching display when combined with Bacopa and, believe it or not, edible strawberries. A lot of my Italian friends usually wait until after Easter to plant amethyst flowers and other plants that love warm soil, including tomatoes.

Planting
Seeding: Direct sow in early spring for summer flowering

Transplanting: Mid-March

Spacing: 8–10"

Growing

Amethyst flower plants will grow well in **partial to full shade**. Flower production and color are best in **partial shade**. The soil should be **fertile** and **well drained**. Add planting mix, peat moss or compost to ensure proper drainage.

Do not cover the seeds when you plant them because they need light to germinate. They will require light watering twice a day as they germinate.

Pinch tips often to encourage new growth and more blooms.

Tips

Grow amethyst flowers in mixed borders, mixed containers or hanging baskets.

These plants can be grown as houseplants year-round or brought indoors at the end of the season. They can be divided and potted for the winter then transplanted in spring when the soil is warm.

Recommended

B. americana (B. elata) is an upright, bushy annual growing 12–24" tall and wide. Blue, white or violet flowers appear in summer. 'Sapphire' is more compact than the species and produces blue flowers with white centers.

B. speciosa forms a bushy mound of foliage. It grows 8–18" tall with an equal or narrower spread and bears white, blue or purple flowers all summer. 'Jingle Bells' series includes 'Blue Bells,' a compact selection with violet blue flowers; 'Marine Bells,' with deep violet blue flowers; and 'Silver Bells,' a compact

selection with white blooms. 'Starlight' forms a compact mound up to 8" high and wide. Its flowers may be light blue, bright blue, purple or white. The 'Troll' series includes 'Blue Troll' and 'White Troll' are compact and bushy, growing about 10" tall.

Problems & Pests

Amethyst flower plants are generally problem free. Whiteflies may cause some trouble but can be controlled with insecticidal soap.

Angelica
Angelica

Height: 3–8' **Spread:** 3–4' **Flower color:** yellow, green, white, purple

WHEN MY DAUGHTER Edie first brought home about 20 roots of this plant I wondered what she was doing. I had always thought of Angelica as a weed. It grows all over the coastal areas of California, and the California Native Plant Association considers it the 'Pampas Grass' of the coast. I have since experienced its leaf stalks as a wonderful asparagus-tasting vegetable. The seeds are also used in some of the finest Northern California wines. Angelica combines beautifully with foxgloves and Hollyhock.

Planting

Seeding: Start freshly ripened seed indoors in fall or direct sow in early spring; can be difficult to grow from seed

Transplanting: Mid-March; best purchased as one-year-old plants from nurseries

Spacing: 2–5'

Growing

Angelica grows well in **full sun** or **partial shade.** The soil should be **fertile** and **moist,** though some drought is tolerated. This plant has a large taproot and resents being moved or divided. Seedlings should be planted while still small and then the plants should not be moved again.

All parts of this edible plant have a licorice scent. The stems are sometimes candied and used to decorate cakes.

This species is a monocarpic perennial, which means that it may live for several years but will die once it has set seed. It is often grown as a biennial. Remove flowerheads before the seed sets to extend the plant's life or allow seeds to set and self-sow to keep a supply of replacement plants growing.

Tips

Angelica's dense clump of attractive, scented foliage and its need for moist soil makes it an excellent choice near a pond or other water feature. If kept well watered, it will thrive in a mixed or herbaceous border or in a woodland garden. It responds well to mulching with compost or well-rotted manure.

Recommended

A. archangelica (Angelica, European Angelica) forms a mound of large, deeply cut foliage. It flowers the second year from seed in early to mid-summer. Yellow-green flowers are borne in large rounded clusters at the tops of tall, strong stems.

The seeds are thought to aid digestion. The roots, dried and ground, can make a tea said to be a liver tonic. Always consult a physician before using.

Baby's Breath
Gypsophila

Height: 12"–4' **Spread:** 12"–4' **Flower color:** white, pink, mauve

IN MY MIND there just isn't a better filler for any bouquet than Baby's Breath, and I have included it in every flower arrangement I have ever made. It does not, however, combine well with all other flowers in the garden. Try it in combination with dwarf dahlias and Alstromeria. Seeding during the growing season will ensure plentiful cut flowers. Harvesting the seedheads will keep plants blooming.

Planting

Seeding: Indoors in late winter; direct sow from mid-spring to early summer

Transplanting: Mid-March; available in six-packs and 4" pots all spring and summer

Spacing: 8–18"

Growing

Baby's Breath grows best in **full sun.** The soil should be of **poor fertility,** and it should be **light, sandy** and **neutral to slightly alkaline,** with a pH between 7.0 and 7.5. A soil test is beneficial; add oyster shell lime or dolomitic lime to acidic soil before planting Baby's Breath. Allow the soil to dry out between waterings.

Don't space the seedlings too far apart. The plants will flower more profusely if slightly crowded, and crowding also offers maximum support for the plants.

Individual plants are short-lived, so sow more seeds every week or two until early summer to encourage a longer blooming period.

G. elegans

The genus name, Gypsophila, *is derived from gypsum and* philos *(loving), a reference to the plants' preference for chalky soils or lime.*

G. paniculata with *Lychnis coronaria* (above)

Tips

The clouds of flowers are ideal for rock gardens, rock walls, mixed containers or for mixing in borders with bold-colored flowers or coarse foliage.

Baby's Breath is native to the northeastern Mediterranean and looks very good in a Mediterranean-style garden.

Recommended

G. elegans forms an upright mound of airy stems, foliage and flowers. The plant grows 12–24" tall. The flowers are usually white but can have pink or purple veining that gives the flowers an overall appearance of color. '**Covent Garden**' has very large white flowers and grows 20–36" tall. '**Gypsy Pink**' bears double or semi-double pink flowers. This compact cultivar grows about 12" tall. '**White Elephant**' has glossy green foliage and large,

pure white flowers about $1/4$" in diameter held in loose clusters. It is an upright grower, growing to 36" tall. It is an excellent choice for arrangements and bouquets.

G. paniculata is a perennial grown as an annual. It grows 36–48" tall and wide. This is the plant the florists use as a bouquet filler. The white flowers are produced in large clusters in mid- to late summer. '**Snow White**' grows 36" tall and has masses of pure white flowers. Sow seed before April for summer blooms.

Problems & Pests

Most common problems are forms of fungal disease and can be avoided by not overwatering the plants and not handling them when they are wet. Leafhoppers can infect plants with aster yellows. When seedlings first sprout, they need protection from slugs and snails.

Baby's Breath makes a wonderful addition to flower bouquets. The sprays of flowers can also be dried and used in fresh or dried arrangements.

Bachelor's Buttons
Cornflower, Basket Flower
Centaurea

Height: 12"–6' **Spread:** 6–36"
Flower color: blue, red, pink, white, violet

COMBINING BACHELOR'S BUTTONS
with nasturtium and *Verbena bonariensis* will
give a garden that wild western look. Adding
Dusty Miller and red geranium will complete the
picture and make your garden a showstopper. All
these plants take the same care with once-a-week
watering, even during hot spells in the Sacramento
Valley. These plants will not be affected by a heavy
deer population, but watch out for rabbits.

*The Latin name
means 'century' and
refers to the folklore
that this plant can
live for a hundred
years—it re-seeds
easily and outgrows
most pest problems.*

Planting
Seeding: Direct sow in early fall for spring
blooms and in spring for summer blooms;
start indoors in late winter

Spacing: 12–24"

Growing
Bachelor's buttons do best in **full sun. Moderate
to fertile, moist, well-drained** soil is preferable,
but any soil is tolerated. Light frost won't harm
the plants.

Tips

Bachelor's buttons work well as filler plants in a mixed border or in a wildflower or cottage-style garden. They are attractive when used in masses or small groups. Bachelor's buttons are often included in packets of mixed annual or wildflower seeds.

Once these plants finish blooming, they are not as attractive. Grow them mixed with other plants—as the bachelor's buttons fade, the other plants can fill in the space they leave. Pull the individual plants right out when their flowering is complete.

Recommended

C. americana (Basket Flower) is an erect plant reaching a height of 36–72" and spreading 30–36". Large rose pink flowers bloom in summer. The flowers of this species close up at night.

C. cyanus (Cornflower, Bachelor's Buttons) is an upright annual that

grows 12–36" tall and spreads 6–24". The flowers are most often blue but can be many shades of red, pink, violet or white. Plants in the '**Boy**' series grow up to 39" tall and have large double flowers in all colors. 'Florence' is a compact dwarf cultivar, 12–18" tall, with flowers in a variety of colors.

Problems & Pests

Aphids, downy mildew and powdery mildew may cause problems.

Bacopa

Sutera

Height: 3–5" **Spread:** 12–20" **Flower color:** white, lavender

I HAVE USED BACOPA with rabbit fern, dwarf impatiens and *Ipomoea batatas* 'Marguerite' crowded into an 18" moss basket. It was a wonderfully successful display that sold very well in the nursery. When used in hanging baskets, Bacopa combines well with Sweet Alyssum, and in my experience, Sweet Alyssum deters whiteflies, which can afflict Bacopa.

Planting

Seeding: Not recommended

Transplanting: Once soil has warmed; transplanting from 4" pots is recommended

Spacing: 12"

Growing

Bacopa grows equally well in **full sun** or **partial shade**. The soil should be of **average fertility, humus rich, moist** and **well drained**. Don't allow this plant to completely dry out; the leaves will die quickly if they become dry. Cut back the dead growth to encourage new shoots to form.

Tips

Bacopa is a popular plant for hanging baskets, mixed containers and window boxes. It will form an attractive spreading mound in a rock garden, but it will need to be watered regularly.

Be careful of the potential confusion between Bacopa monnieri, *which is a tropical aquatic plant, and the* Bacopa *belonging to the* Sutera *genus.* Sutera cordata *is the Bacopa most often found in nurseries.*

Recommended

S. cordata is a compact, trailing plant. It bears small white flowers all summer. **'Lavender Showers'** forms a dense mound of heart-shaped leaves with scalloped edges and bears tiny, star-shaped, lavender flowers along the neat, trailing stems. **'Olympic Gold'** has gold-variegated foliage and bears white flowers. **'Snowflake,'** one of the first cultivars available, bears white flowers. **'Giant Snowflake'** is a more vigorous and hardy development of 'Snowflake.'

Problems & Pests

Whiteflies and other small insects can become a real menace on this plant, because the tiny leaves and dense growth create perfect hiding spots for small insects.

Begonia
Fibrous Begonia, Wax Begonia
Begonia

Height: 6–12" **Spread:** 6–12" **Flower color:** pink, white, red, yellow, orange, bicolored

ALTHOUGH BEGONIA can be a perennial in many parts of Northern California, it is at its best during its first year. Begonia plants are at home in any garden, and all are self-grooming. My daughter Edie took over the moss basket business from me and included wonderful, colorful Begonia plants in many of her creations.

Planting
Seeding: Indoors in early winter
Transplanting: After mid-March
Spacing: 6–12"

Growing

Begonia plants prefer **light or partial shade,** although some of the new varieties of wax begonia are sun tolerant if the soil is kept moist. The soil should be **fertile,** rich in **organic matter, well drained** and with a **neutral to slightly acidic pH.** Allow the soil to dry out slightly between waterings and always check soil moisture prior to watering. If you can form the soil into a ball, watering is not required. If it crumbles, watering is necessary.

Begonia plants can be tricky to grow from seed. The seeds require light to germinate (do not cover). Keep the soil surface moist but not soggy, and maintain daytime temperature at 70–80° F and night temperature above 50° F. The plants can be potted individually once they have three or four leaves.

Tips

Begonia is useful for shaded garden beds and planters. The plant's neat rounded habit makes it attractive as an edging plant. It can also be paired with roses and geraniums for a formal look. The new varieties can be used where other begonias will burn out in the sun. You can have a continuous border from the shady part of your garden to the sunny part.

Recommended

B. semperflorens produces pink, white, red or bicolored flowers and green, bronze, reddish or variegated white foliage. Most plants in this species grow 6–12" tall and wide. **'Ambassador'** series is heat tolerant

and has dark green leaves and white, pink or red flowers. **'Senator'** series is also heat tolerant, and has bronze leaves and red, pink or white flowers. The cultivars **'Varsity'** and **'Rio'** are similar to the above series but do not tolerate full sun in areas such as the Sacramento Valley. They are best kept in areas where there is only morning sun.

Problems & Pests

To prevent fungal problems, ensure good air circulation and water only in the morning. Problems with mealybugs, whiteflies, leaf spot and stem rot can occur. Mulching with peat moss will discourage stem rot and other soil-borne organisms.

Bells-of-Ireland

Moluccella

Height: 24–36" **Spread:** 9" **Flower color:** green

THE BRIGHT TO PALE GREEN of the wonderful Bells-of-Ireland makes a great contrast to a bed of *Lobelia* 'Crystal Palace'. Bells-of-Ireland plants are great self-seeders. In the Sacramento Valley they should be grown in an area that receives only morning sun.

Planting

Seeding: Indoors in mid-winter; direct sow in mid-spring for summer flowers or in late summer for fall flowers

Transplanting: March to April

Spacing: 12"

Growing

Bells-of-Ireland prefers **full sun** but tolerates partial shade. The soil should be of **average or good fertility, moist** and **well drained**. When seeding, don't cover the seeds because they need light to germinate. Water seeds twice a day until they start sprouting.

The tall stems of Bells-of-Ireland plants may need staking in windy locations. Harvesting the blooms regularly will shorten the plant, eliminating the need for staking.

Tips

Use Bells-of-Ireland at the back of a border—the green spikes create an interesting backdrop for more brightly colored flowers.

Bells-of-Ireland is popular in fresh or dried flower arrangements. When hung upside down to dry, the green cups turn white or beige with a papery texture.

Recommended

M. laevis is an upright plant that bears spikes of creamy white, inconspicuous flowers. The interesting feature of these plants is the large, green, shell-like cup that encircles each flower. The species is generally grown and cultivars are rarely offered.

Contrary to what the name implies, these plants are native to the Middle East, not to Ireland.

The greenish bells are actually enlarged sepals, while the rest of the flower is inside and is very small.

Bird's Eyes
Gilia

Height: 12–20" **Spread:** 8–10" **Flower color:** light to dark purple; purple-dotted, yellow to orange throats

BIRD'S EYES is a cool weather annual and not recommended for summer planting in the interior valleys of California. In all areas it makes a wonder show in late fall and early spring with lacy foliage and bright blue flowers. In bouquets, the flowers are used much like Baby's Breath. They also are good for dried arrangements, combining well with dry Eucalyptus branches.

Planting

Seeding: Direct sow in fall or early spring

Transplanting: Not recommended

Spacing: 8"

Growing

Bird's Eyes prefers **full sun**. The soil should be **light** and **well drained**. Thin the seedlings to prevent overcrowding.

Tips

Bird's Eyes is native to California and is quite at home in a wild or naturalized garden. It also works well in an annual bed or mixed border. Bird's Eyes does not require a lot of water.

Recommended

G. tricolor is a slender, mound-forming plant with finely dissected leaves. The flowers bloom from late spring to late summer.

Problems & Pests

Rust and powdery mildew may cause problems. Watering in the morning only or using drip irrigation should avoid any mildew problems.

The flowers look like the eyes of a little bird, thus giving rise to the common name.

Black-Eyed Susan

Coneflower, Gloriosa Daisy

Rudbeckia

Height: 10–36" **Spread:** 12–18" **Flower color:** yellow, orange, red, sometimes bicolored; brown or green centers

THE MORE THE BLOOMS OF BLACK-EYED SUSAN are cut, the more they will flower, and the sturdier the plant will grow. Red salvias, light blue Lobelia and Sweet Alyssum are wonderful companion plants. In California Black-eyed Susan thrives in the most inhospitable soils as long as it is watered sufficiently.

Black-eyed Susan is a colorful plant native to the Midwest. It makes an excellent addition to wildflower and natural gardens.

Planting

Seeding: Indoors in late winter; direct sow in mid-spring

Transplanting: Mid-March through April; from six-packs

Spacing: 18"

Growing

Black-eyed Susan grows equally well in **full sun** and **partial shade**. The soil should be of **average fertility, humus rich, moist** and **well drained**. This plant tolerates heavy clay soils and hot weather.

Mulching in mid-July will increase bloom production.

This is a short-lived perennial that is grown as an annual. It is not worth trying to keep over winter because it grows and flowers quickly from seed. If it is growing in loose, moist soil, this plant may self-seed.

R. hirta

This tough plant has long-lasting blooms that keep fall flowerbeds bright.

'Gloriosa Daisy' (above)

'Gloriosa Daisy' (below)

Tips

Black-eyed Susan can be planted individually or in groups. Use this flower in beds and borders, large containers, meadow plantings and wildflower gardens. The plants will bloom well, even in the hottest part of the garden.

Keep cutting the flowers to promote more blooming. Black-eyed Susan makes a long-lasting vase flower.

Recommended

R. hirta forms a bristly mound of foliage. In summer and fall, it bears bright yellow, daisy-like flowers with brown centers. **'Gloriosa Daisy'** has large flowers, up to 6" across, in warm shades of gold and brown. The plants grow up to 36" tall. **'Indian Summer'** has huge flowers, 6–9" across, on sturdy plants that grow 36" tall or taller. **'Irish Eyes'** has single flowers with green centers.

The plants grow up to 30" tall. 'Toto' is a dwarf cultivar that grows 10–12" tall. This cultivar is small enough to include in planters.

Problems & Pests

Good air circulation around plants will help prevent fungal diseases such as powdery mildew and downy mildew. Aphids and rust can cause problems.

Insects find it difficult to climb up the hairy stems of Black-eyed Susan plants.

'Irish Eyes' (center)

Black-Eyed Susan Vine
Thunbergia

Height: 5' or more **Spread:** equal to height, if trained **Flower color:** yellow, orange, cream white; dark centers

BLACK-EYED SUSAN VINE is very effective if several plants are transplanted into a 12–14" basket. The plants will hang down 3' to 6' with profuse blooms all over the plant. One of my favorite uses for this planting method is to hide old dead trees. I once used Black-eyed Susan Vine to cover an old tree trunk until I had the trunk removed a year later.

Planting

Seeding: Indoors in mid-winter; direct sow in mid-spring

Transplanting: Mid-April

Spacing: 12–18"

Growing

Black-eyed Susan Vine grows well in **full sun, partial shade** or **light shade.** Grow it in **fertile, moist** and **well-drained** soil that is high in **organic matter.**

This plant can be brought into the house over winter and returned to the garden the following spring—it is a perennial treated as an annual. Where winters are cold and wet, it is better to start off with new plants each year.

Tips

Black-eyed Susan Vine can be trained to twine around fences and walls as well as up trees and over shrubs. It is also attractive trailing down from the top of a rock garden or rock wall or growing in mixed containers and hanging baskets.

These vines can be quite vigorous and may need to be trimmed back from time to time.

The vines are, for the most part, disease free but require a steady supply of fertilizer. Most growers use time-released fertilizers in hanging baskets. I usually use either compost tea or alfalfa tea.

Recommended

T. alata is a vigorous, twining climber. It bears yellow flowers, often with dark centers, in summer and fall. 'Susie' is a commonly

found series with large flowers in yellow, orange or white.

Alternate Species

T. gregorii (*T. gibsonii*) (Orange Clock Vine) is a twining, climbing perennial that will climb 6–7' when grown as an annual. It can be used as a climber or as a groundcover. Use 3' spacing when training up a trellis or wall and 5' spacing when using as groundcover. Bright orange flowers are produced in summer, sometimes to the first frost.

Blanket Flower
Gaillardia

Height: 12"–4' **Spread:** 12–24" **Flower color:** red, orange or yellow, often in combination

MY GRANDFATHER, born in Missouri, came to California where he married my grandmother. One of the wedding presents they received was a small packet of blanket flower seeds harvested from Missouri. My grandmother kept those plants and the seeds and grew them everywhere they moved, including the mountains, valleys and coastal regions of our state. She grew them even after my grandfather's death.

Planting
Seeding: Indoors in late winter; direct sow from mid-April through June

Transplanting: Mid-March through mid-April; from six-packs, 4" pots or one-gallon containers

Spacing: 12"

Growing
Blanket flowers prefer **full sun**. The soil should be of **poor or average fertility, light, sandy** and **well drained**. The seeds require light and warm soil to germinate. Water the plants lightly two to three times a day until the seeds sprout.

Once rooted, they require less water.
When the first true leaves appear,
they need deep watering only once a
week. Deadhead to encourage more
blooms.

Tips

Use blanket flowers in an informal
cottage garden, mixed border or on
exposed, sunny slopes. Plant blanket
flowers in a location where they will
not get watered with other plants.

Recommended

G. aristata is a perennial best grown
as an annual. It reaches a height of
24–30" and spreads 18–24". Yellow or
red, often two-toned, flowers with
reddish orange centers bloom from
summer to fall. 'Choice Mix' has
eight different strains mixed together.
The plants grow 12–26" tall. Large 4"
diameter blooms come in yellow to
wine red to dark golden brown, with
dark red to yellow centers.

G. x *grandiflora* is a bushy perennial
that works very well as an annual. It
grows 24–48" tall and spreads
18–24". The aster-like flowers are
red, orange and yellow with yellow-
brown to reddish centers. 'Baby
Cole' grows to 8" tall; the bright
orange and red flowers have yellow
tips and reddish centers. 'Burgundy'
('Burgunder') grows 24" tall and has
deep burgundy red flowers. 'Kobold'
('Goblin') reaches 12" tall and has
large, yellow-tipped, deep red flowers
with deep red centers. 'Tokajer'
grows 30" tall and bears bright, deep
orange flowers. 'Torchlight' also
grows to 30" and has yellow flowers
bordered with red.

G. x *grandiflora* (above), *G. pulchella* (below)

G. pulchella forms a basal rosette of
leaves. The red flowers have yellow
tips and centers in shades of red,
orange, yellow, purple and brown.
The plants grow 18–36" tall and
12–24" wide. 'Plume' series has double flowerheads in vibrant shades of
red or yellow. It grows about 12" tall,
with an equal spread, and has a uniform dwarf growth habit and long
blooming time. 'Red Plume' has
deep red double flowers.

Problems & Pests

Possible problems include powdery
mildew, leafhoppers, bacterial and
fungal leaf spot and rust.

Blue Lace Flower
Trachymene

Height: 24" **Spread:** 8–12" **Flower color:** light blue, white

BLUE LACE FLOWER is an ideal flowering annual for coastal climates. In the Sacramento Valley it is best used as a winter-blooming annual. I love this wonderful flower for any cut-flower bed. When it grows too leggy, just cut more bouquets. It is a native of Australia and is deer resistant.

Planting

Seeding: Direct sow in April on the coast; in late August to September in the interior valleys

Spacing: 12"

Growing

Blue Lace Flower prefers a **sheltered location** in **full sun** that isn't too hot. It enjoys **cool night** temperatures. The soil should be of **average fertility, light** and **well drained**.

Sowing the seeds directly into the garden is preferable because the seedlings dislike having their roots disturbed. The seeds can be slow to germinate if the ground is cool. If you do start them indoors, sow the seeds in individual peat pots in late winter. Don't cover the seeds; they need light to germinate.

Insert forked branches around young plants to keep them from flopping over in rain and wind.

Tips

Blue Lace Flower is used in beds and borders, usually combined with other plants. The plants are quite erect, and with their delicate, feathery foliage they look good in an informal cottage-style garden. The flowers are long lasting when used in fresh flower arrangements.

Recommended

T. coerulea (Didiscus coeruleus) is a delicate, upright plant that bears light blue, scented flowers. 'Lace Veil' is a cultivar that bears fragrant, white flowers.

Butterfly Weed
Asclepias

Height: 18–36" **Spread:** 12–24" **Flower color:** orange, yellow, red

BUTTERFLY WEED mixes well with tall perennials such as Mexican Sage and Butterfly Bush. This wonderful plant adds a striking orange or yellow accent to any area of the garden, especially areas for attracting butterflies. A planting of parsley at the base of Butterfly Weed helps attract Monarchs, Swallowtails and many other varieties of butterflies.

The genus name, Asclepias, is derived from Asklepios, the Greek god of medicine, referring to the plant's reputed medicinal properties.

Planting

Seeding: Sow fresh seed in cold frame in early spring

Transplanting: Mid-March to mid-April

Spacing: 12–24"

Growing

Butterfly Weed prefers **full sun**. Any **well-drained** soil is tolerated, and **moderate to infertile** soil will help keep the plant from overgrowing its place. This plant is drought tolerant.

Butterfly Weed with perennials (below)

Tips

Use Butterfly Weed in meadow plantings, borders, on dry banks, in neglected areas and in wildflower, cottage and butterfly gardens. It makes an excellent cut flower.

Butterfly Weed is a major food source for the Monarch butterfly and will attract butterflies to your garden. The Monarch lays its eggs on the stems and leaves of the related species *A. speciosa.*

Recommended

A. tuberosa forms a clump of upright, leafy stems. It bears clusters of orange flowers. 'Gay Butterflies' bears orange, yellow or red flowers.

Problems & Pests

Aphids and mealybugs can be problems on rare occasions.

The bold orange blooms of Butterfly Weed work well as cut flowers, and the seedpods add attractive color in fall.

California Poppy
Eschscholzia

Height: 8–18" **Spread:** 8–18"
Flower color: orange, yellow, red; less commonly pink, apricot, cream

I CAN STILL REMEMBER the many family trips we took from Mendocino County in Northern California to Sacramento. As we wound our way through the foothills into the valley every June, we were treated to a magnificent display of orange California Poppy (my favorite color of these plants) and the native blue Lupine. The area no longer affords such beauty, but it is forever etched in my mind's eye.

Planting

Seeding: Direct sow mid-October or after first rains; water if it doesn't rain within two weeks

Spacing: 6–12"

Growing

California Poppy prefers **full sun** but tolerates some shade. The soil should be of **poor or average fertility** and **well drained**. With too rich a soil, the plants will be lush and green but will bear few, if any, flowers.

California Poppy requires a lot of water for germination and development of young plants. Until they flower, provide the plants with regular and frequent watering. Once they begin flowering, they are more drought tolerant.

Never start this plant indoors because it dislikes having its roots disturbed. California Poppy will sprout quickly when planted directly in the garden. Start seeds in early fall for blooms in spring or in early spring for blooms later in summer.

The genus name honors Johann Eschscholz (1793–1831), a Russian botanist.

One successful technique is to seed into one-gallon containers in good potting mix. Once the seeds have sprouted, set the whole container into the ground and make sure it doesn't dry out. Timing of seeding is important.

Tips

California Poppy can be included in an annual border or annual planting in a cottage garden. This plant self-seeds wherever it is planted; it is perfect for naturalizing in a meadow garden or rock garden, where it will come back year after year.

Recommended

E. californica forms a mound of delicate, feathery, blue-green foliage and bears satiny, orange or yellow flowers all summer. The species

Though they have little nutritional value, the petals of California Poppy can be eaten and will brighten up an everyday salad.

grows 8–18". '**Ballerina**' has a mixture of colors and semi-double or double flowers. '**Chiffon**' forms compact plants, up to 8", that bear semi-double flowers in pink and apricot. '**Mission Bells**' bears ruffled double and semi-double flowers in mixed and solid shades of orange, yellow, red, cream and pink. '**Thai Silk**' bears flowers in pink, red, yellow and orange with silky, wavy-edged petals. The compact plants grow 8–10" tall.

Problems & Pests

California Poppy generally has few pest problems but may be troubled by fungi occasionally if overwatered. The flowers may also show signs of powdery mildew.

Candytuft
Iberis

Height: 12–15" **Spread:** 6–9" or more **Flower color:** white, pink, purple, red

I LOVE TO USE CANDYTUFT plants in rock gardens that need a summertime facelift. They were among my favorite blooming plants in my mother's garden in Loomis. When the perennials started to peter out in the hot Sacramento Valley, candytufts provided a wonderful addition of blooms.

Candytuft needs to be sheared lightly after every bloom cycle to promote new growth and more flowers.

Planting

Seeding: Indoors in late winter; outdoors around last frost

Transplanting: Mid-March to mid-April for best results

Spacing: 6"

Growing

Candytufts prefer to grow in **full sun.** The soil should be of **poor or average fertility, well drained** and have a **neutral or alkaline pH.**

Tips

These informal plants can be used on rock walls, in mixed containers or to edge beds. They are not as popular as the perennial candytuft *(I. sempervirens)* but should be used more often.

Recommended

I. amara (Rocket Candytuft, Hyacinth-flowered Candytuft) is an erect annual growing 12–15" tall and 6" wide. Clusters of fragrant purplish white to white flowers are produced in summer. The flower clusters look like those of hyacinths.

I. umbellata (Globe Candytuft) is a bushy, mound-forming annual with flowers in shades of pink, purple, red or white. The plant grows 12–15" tall and spreads 9" or more. **'Dwarf Fairy'** ('Dwarf Fairyland') is a compact plant that bears many flowers in a variety of pastel shades.

Problems & Pests

Keep an eye open for slugs and snails. Caterpillars can also be a problem. In poorly drained soil, fungal problems may develop.

I. umbellata (this page)

A side dressing of organic fertilizer will improve blooming.

Canterbury Bells
Cup-and-Saucer Plant
Campanula

Height: 18–36" **Spread:** 12" **Flower color:** blue, purple, pink, white

WHEN I WAS ABOUT SIX YEARS OLD, I was at my grandparents' home, and I thought a bouquet of my grandmother's wonderful Canterbury Bells would make a great present for my mother. I harvested a whole bundle of them and gave them to my mother. She was delighted, but my grandmother wasn't. I later found out that my grandmother had saved the seed for these flowers from her neighbor's garden before the neighbor pulled them out and threw them away.

Planting

Seeding: Indoors in mid-winter or direct sow in late spring; directly seeded plants will not flower until the following season

Transplanting: October in all but the coldest areas, mid-April in the coldest areas; best from six-packs or 4" pots

Spacing: 12–18"

Growing

Canterbury Bells prefers **full sun** but tolerates partial shade. The soil should be **fertile, moist** and **well drained**. This plant will not suffer if the weather cools or if there is a light frost.

When sowing, leave seeds uncovered because they require light for germination. Harden off in a cold frame or on a sheltered porch before planting out. Canterbury Bells transplants easily, even when in full bloom.

Canterbury Bells is a biennial treated as an annual, which is why the plants must be started early in the year. If they are started too late, they will not flower the first year.

Tips

Planted in small groups, Canterbury Bells looks attractive in a border or rock garden. The tallest varieties produce good flowers for cutting. Use dwarf varieties in planters.

Canterbury Bells looks good in a cottage garden or other informal garden where its habit of re-seeding can keep it growing year after year.

Recommended

C. medium forms a basal rosette of foliage. The pink, blue, white or purple cup-shaped flowers are borne on tall spikes. The plant grows 24–36" tall and spreads about 12". **'Bells of Holland'** is a dwarf cultivar. It has flowers in various colors and grows about 18" tall. **'Champion'** is a true annual cultivar, flowering much sooner from seed than the species or other cultivars. Blue or pink flowers are available.

Problems & Pests

Slugs and snails are fond of Canterbury Bells. Occasional problems with aphids, crown rot, leaf spot, powdery mildew and rust are also possible.

The genus name, Campanula, *means 'little bell,' a reference to the shape of the flowers.*

Canterbury Bells is an old 'English Cottage Garden' favorite that works well with many plantings of a similar nature, such as the Clematis x jackmanii *shown at right.*

Cape Marigold
African Daisy
Dimorphotheca

Height: 12–18" **Spread:** 12" **Flower color:** white, orange, yellow, pink; often with black, brown, orange or purple centers

A SEPTEMBER SOWING of the seeds of these plants will produce masses of winter and spring color on rocky hillsides. Cape marigolds are great colorful additions to any landscape and can be used effectively as fill plants until groundcovering shrubs mature and take over.

Planting

Seeding: Indoors in early spring; direct sow after last frost

Transplanting: Mid-March through summer

Spacing: 12"

Growing

Cape marigolds like to grow in **full sun**. The soil should be **light, fertile** and **well drained**. These plants are drought resistant. In heavy clay soils they may damp off with too much water. Always check soil moisture before watering. Mulching in mid-summer will cut down on the plants' water needs.

Cape marigolds do not grow well in rainy weather, and overwatering will harm the plants. Plant under the eaves of the house, in window boxes or raised beds to protect them from too much rain.

Tips

Cape marigolds are most attractive when planted in groups or masses. Use them in beds and borders. The flowers close at night and on cloudy days, so although they can be cut for flower arrangements, they might close if the vase isn't getting enough light.

'Salmon Queen' (above)

These plants need to be sheared back after every bloom cycle to maintain their compactness.

Recommended

D. pluvialis (Cape Marigold; Rainy Daisy) has white flowers with purple on the undersides and bases of the petals. **'Glistening White'** is a compact plant that bears large, pure white flowers with black centers.

D. **'Salmon Queen'** bears salmon and apricot pink flowers on plants that spread to about 18".

D. pluvialis (center), *D. sinuata* (below)

D. sinuata (Star of the Veldt) forms a 12–18" mound. It bears yellow, orange, white or pink daisy-like flowers all summer. Cultivars with larger flowers are available.

D. **'Starshine'** is a low, mound-forming cultivar with shiny flowers in pink, orange, white or red, with yellow centers.

Problems & Pests

Fungal problems are likely to occur in hot and wet locations. Dry, cool places produce healthy plants that are less susceptible to disease.

You may find cape marigolds listed as either Dimorphotheca *or* Osteospermum. Osteospermum *is a closely related genus that is more commonly grown in Britain.*

Cathedral Bells
Cup-and-Saucer Vine
Cobaea

Height: 15–25' in hot summer areas; 6' in cool summer areas
Spread: variable **Flower color:** purple, white

WHEN I FIRST RAN ACROSS CATHEDRAL BELLS at the Luther Burbank
Gardens in Santa Rosa, I didn't have the foggiest idea what it was. Since that
time this plant has become exceptionally popular because it is easy to grow,
covers a large area and blooms wonderfully all summer long. At Luther Burbank Gardens it was not given adequate sunlight so it never quite reached its
potential. When I became more familiar with the plant, I suggested giving it
more sun. It has become very successful, and seeds from the plant are now
sold in the gift shop. I love to mix different vines of Cathedral Bells in the
same planting hole for interesting effects. This plant combines well with
Ipomoea tricolor (Morning Glory) and climbing nasturtium.

Planting

Seeding: Indoors in mid-winter

Transplanting: Mid-April to June in warm soil

Spacing: 12"

Growing

Cathedral Bells prefers **full sun.** The soil should be **well drained** and of **average fertility.** You will need to notch seeds with a knife and press them edgewise into a moistened planting mix.

Tips

This plant is fond of hot weather and will do best if planted in a sheltered site with southern exposure. Grow up a trellis, over an arbor or along a chain-link fence. Cathedral Bells requires a sturdy support in order to climb. It uses grabbing hooks to climb so won't be able to grow up a wall without something to grab hold of. It can be trained to fill almost any space.

Recommended

C. scandens is a vigorous climbing vine originally from Mexico. Its flowers are creamy green when they open and mature to deep purple. **Var.** *alba* has white flowers.

Problems & Pests

This plant may have trouble with aphids.

This interesting vine has sweetly scented flowers that are a cream color with a green tinge when they open; the flowers darken to purple as they age.

Chickabiddy
Climbing Snapdragon
Asarina

Height: 3–8' **Spread:** 24" **Flower color:** red, blue, purple, pink, white

CHICKABIDDY PLANTS are spectacular vines when allowed to sprawl. They make a wonderful groundcover and have lovely foliage and flowers closely resembling those of their close relative, the snapdragon. Chicka-biddies are great additions to a hanging basket when combined with other colorful trailing annuals such as black-eyed Susan vine. I had these plants in the nursery in Belvedere. Because of the unique flowers the plants sold immediately, and when I went to reorder, the grower was out and never grew them again. Chickabiddies are now available at several local seed companies such as Renee's Garden.

Planting

Seeding: Indoors in late winter or early spring

Transplanting: Mid-March to the end of April

Spacing: 18–24"

Growing

Chickabiddies prefer **light shade** but tolerate partial shade if protected from the hot afternoon sun. The soil should be **fertile, light, sandy** and **well drained.** In excessively hot and sunny locations, these plants may wilt and suffer leaf burn.

Tips

Chickabiddies make an interesting change from impatiens in shady hanging baskets. They can also be used as groundcovers, trailing along the ground and over any objects they encounter. They are easily trained to grow up a trellis or any structure they can wind their tendrils around. Try them under shrubs and in shaded rock gardens.

Chickabiddy plants can be grown from root cuttings. In mountain areas where the ground freezes, cut the plant back to 3' and dig up the entire root. Store in damp peat moss in a cool area, not below freezing, for replanting the following spring. In areas where the ground does not freeze, mulch with 3" of insulating material.

Recommended

A. antirrhiniflora (Maurandella antirrhiniflora) is a twining climber growing 3–6' tall. It is a perennial treated as an annual in our area.

These plants are related to snapdragons, but they lack the hinged part of the flower that opens the mouth of the 'dragon.'

The flowers are usually purple, but cultivation has produced a range of colors including pink, red and blue. All flowers have yellow markings in the throat.

A. scandens is a vigorous, twining climber growing 4–8' tall. It flowers quickly from seed, producing purple, pink or white flowers in late spring to late summer. Many plants sold under the name *A. scandens* are actually *A. erubescens.* Cultivars may be listed under either name. 'Jewel' mix bears flowers in a variety of colors. 'Joan Loraine' has purple flowers with white throats.

China Aster

Callistephus

Height: 6–30" **Spread:** 6–18" **Flower color:** purple, blue, pink, red, white, peach, yellow

WITH THE LARGE SELECTION of interesting flower shapes, different heights and great colors, China Aster plants make a wonderful display by themselves in a bed. Add an extra touch and edge the bed with white Sweet Alyssum or annual candytuft. I ran into trouble with China Aster plants once when I put them in the Sonoma County Fair flower show. The humidity of the building along with the heat melted them within a week, so I had to replace them. They prefer to grow in hot sun in soil that's on the dry side and has excellent drainage. I have found that they can be grown successfully in any area of Northern California as long as these requirements are met.

Planting

Seeding: Indoors in late winter; direct sow after last frost

Transplanting: April or early May in warm soil

Spacing: 6–12"

Growing

China Aster prefers **full sun** but tolerates partial shade. The soil should be **fertile, evenly moist to a little dry** and **well drained**. A pH that is **neutral or alkaline** is preferable. In gardens where the soil is acidic, grow smaller varieties in pots so the soil can be adjusted more easily. Plant in a location sheltered from the wind.

Start seeds in peat pots or peat pellets, because these plants don't like having their roots disturbed. When purchasing plants, select those that are not root-bound. Gently break up the rootball for the best results.

Tips

China Aster is popular because the flowers put on a bright display when planted in groups. There is a wide range of flower types and colors to choose from, within three height groups: dwarf, medium and tall. Use the smaller varieties as edging plants and the taller varieties for cut flowers. Tall varieties may require staking.

Recommended

C. chinensis is the parent of many varieties and cultivars. '**Erfurter**' ('Erfurter Zwerg') is a compact plant growing to 10". Its large, 2 1/2–3" diameter flowers in pink, purple and white bloom from midsummer to fall. It is a good choice for bordering paths and patios. '**Matsumoto**' grows to 30" and bears yellow-centered, semi-double flowers. It resists wilt diseases and can be planted in exposed sites. '**Pot 'n' Patio**' is a popular dwarf cultivar that has double flowers and grows

6–8" tall, with an equal spread. '**Princess**' grows up to 24" tall and bears double or semi-double quilled flowers in a range of colors.

Problems & Pests

Wilt diseases and aster yellows can be prevented by planting China Aster in different locations each year and by planting resistant varieties. Keep China Aster away from Pot Marigold, which hosts insects and diseases potentially harmful to China Aster. Aphids are the most likely insect pests.

Chinese Forget-Me-Not
Cynoglossum

Height: 12–24" **Spread:** to 12" **Flower color:** blue

CHINESE FORGET-ME-NOT is a wonderful self-seeding 'weed' that dies out during the summer heat. It grows anywhere but prefers soil that is well drained but kept moist. I have seen it grow on mossy banks in the shade with color lasting well into summer. It is what I refer to as a dependable annual in that it lasts for only one season. I find that most convenient when I want to replant something else in its place. One of my favorite combinations is the perennial Sweet Violet *(Viola odorata)* and Chinese Forget-me-not.

Planting

Seeding: Indoors in early spring; direct sow in late spring

Transplanting: Around last frost

Spacing: 12"

Growing

Chinese Forget-me-not prefers **full sun** to **partial shade**. The soil should be of **average fertility, moist** and **well drained**. A heavy clay or overly fertile soil will cause floppy, unattractive growth. Use alfalfa pellets to loosen the soil.

Tips

Chinese Forget-me-not can be used in difficult areas. The coarse foliage of the plants is not exceptionally attractive, and the plants look best when mass planted or used to fill in the space under shrubs and other tall border plants. They may re-seed themselves in loose rock walls and other out-of-the-way spots. They will produce a lot of color during the winter doldrums.

This plant self-seeds quite readily and will return for many seasons. Be careful that it doesn't over-take your garden. Removing the flowerheads right before they seed will keep the self-seeding tendencies under control.

Recommended

C. amabile forms an upright plant that branches strongly and bears bright blue flowers in small clusters in spring to early summer. '**Blue Showers**' grows about 24" tall and bears attractive, light blue flowers. '**Firmament**' ('Firmament Blue') is a compact variety, about 12–18" tall, with hairy gray leaves. The pendulous flowers are sky blue.

Problems & Pests

Chinese Forget-me-not is subject to root and stem rot and mildew. Avoid watering in the evening and do not overwater.

The genus name, Cynoglossum, *is from the Greek* kyon *(dog) and* glossum *(tongue), referring to the shape of the plant's leaves.*

Coleus

Solenostemon (Coleus)

Height: 6–24" **Spread:** usually equal to height **Flower color:** light purple; plant grown for foliage

COLEUS USED TO BE CONSIDERED A HOUSEPLANT that required a lot of protection from inclement weather if grown outside. I saw this plant used as one of the major color segments in the gardens at the San Francisco World's Fair in 1939. At the time I was amazed that this very sensitive house-plant could be used outside. Now, you can buy Coleus in six-packs in any nursery in the spring and add them to your flower garden for color.

Planting

Seeding: Indoors in winter

Transplanting: Mid-March through summer; from six-packs or 4" pots

Spacing: 12"

Growing

Coleus prefers to grow in **light or partial shade.** Many varieties of this wonderful plant tolerate full sun in most parts of the state, including along the coast. Coleus tolerates partial shade in warmer parts of the Sacramento Valley, provided it is watered regularly. The plants can grow in full shade as long as it is not too dark. The soil should be **moist, well drained,** of **rich or average fertility** and with lots of **organic matter** added in.

Place the seeds in a refrigerator for one or two days before planting them on the soil surface; the cold temperatures will assist in breaking the seeds' dormancy. They need light to germinate. Seedlings will be green at first, but leaf variegation will develop as the plants mature.

Coleus is easy to propagate from stem cuttings, and in doing so you can ensure that you have a group of plants with the same leaf markings, shapes or colors. As your seedlings develop, decide which you like best, and when they are about three pairs of leaves high, pinch off the tip. The plants will begin to branch out. Pinch all the tips off regularly as the branches grow. This process will produce a very bushy plant from which you will be able to take a large number of cuttings.

The cuttings should be about three leaf pairs long. Make the cut just below a leaf pair, then remove the two bottom leaves. Plant the cuttings in pots filled with a soil mix intended for starting seeds. Keep the soil moist but not soggy. The plants should develop roots within a couple of weeks. Because all of the plants are from a single original plant, they will all have the same markings and color.

Tips

The bold, colorful foliage makes Coleus dramatic when the plants are grouped together as edging plants or in beds, borders or mixed containers. The colors of the foliage can fade in bright sun, so choose the lighter yellow and gold-leaved varieties, which don't fade as much, for sunny spots. Coleus can also be grown indoors as a houseplant in a bright room.

When flower buds develop, it is best to pinch them off, because the plants tend to stretch out and are less attractive after they flower.

Recommended

S. scutellarioides (*Coleus blumei* var. *verschaffeltii*) forms a bushy mound of foliage. The leaf edges range from slightly toothed to very ruffled. The leaves are usually multi-colored with

Coleus can be trained to grow into a standard (tree) form. Pinch off the side branches as they grow. Once the plant reaches the desired height, pinch from the top.

shades ranging from pale greenish yellow to deep purple-black. Dozens of cultivars are available in different sizes. Many cannot be started from seed. A few interesting cultivars that can be started from seed are the 'Dragon' series, with bright yellow-green margins on the variably colored leaves; 'Palisandra,' with velvety, purple black foliage; 'Scarlet Poncho,' with wine red leaves edged in yellow green; and the 'Wizard' series, with large, heart-shaped leaves on compact, 12–14" plants.

Problems & Pests

Slugs and snails can destroy foliage all year long. Mealybugs, scale insects, aphids and whiteflies can cause occasional trouble, and earwigs can destroy a plant overnight. Check for insects when you purchase the plants, especially in spring.

Coreopsis
Tickseed
Coreopsis

Height: 8–4' **Spread**: 8–18" **Flower color:** yellow, red, orange, brown

THESE REWARDING ANNUALS CAN ADD COLOR to a difficult spot in the garden or on a hillside. Coreopsis varieties combine well with many California native flowers. For a wild-looking garden, combine coreopsis with Sunflower, baby's breath, Love-in-a-mist, Corn Cockle and cosmos.

Planting
Seeding: Indoors in mid-winter; direct sow after last frost

Transplanting: After last frost

Spacing: 8–12"

Growing

Coreopsis plants prefer **full sun**. The soil should be of **rich or average fertility, light** and **well drained**. Poor soil is also tolerated but with somewhat reduced flowering. Coreopsis plants should be sown in dry soil and watered well until the first true leaves appear.

Good drainage is the most important factor for these drought-tolerant plants. In the clay soils of Northern California, mix two parts soil and one part commercial planting mix in the top six inches of soil. Mature coreopsis plants benefit from mulching.

Tips

Try coreopsis plants in front of a rustic wooden fence or repeating in clusters in a bed of perennials. These plants are well suited to naturalized meadow plantings and can be used in informal beds and borders where they flower all season if deadheaded regularly. Coreopsis plants also yield lovely cut flowers.

Coreopsis plants can be blown over or have their stems broken during heavy rain or high winds.

A relative of the sunflower, Coreopsis is worth planting for the cheerful sight of the spring flowers. Coreopsis is Greek for 'bug,' a reference to the small, dry, flat seeds that look like insects.

The fine foliage isn't dense enough to hide tomato or peony cages, so insert twiggy branches for the seedlings to grow between for support. In very windy spots, it is best to use a dwarf form of coreopsis. If for some reason the entire bed of coreopsis is blown down, cut the plants back drastically to 3–4" above the soil and add fertilizer and water. The established root system will allow the plants to recover and re-bloom in a few weeks.

Recommended

C. grandiflora is a clump-forming perennial that is best treated as an annual. It grows 18–36" tall, spreads about 18" and bears bright yellow single flowers all summer. This species often self-seeds. **'Early Sunrise'** bears bright yellow double flowers on compact plants that grow about 18" tall.

C. grandiflora (above), 'Early Sunrise' (below)

C. tinctoria forms a clump of basal leaves and tall, branching stems with just a few leaves. It grows up to 4' tall and spreads up to 18". The flowers are usually bright yellow with dark red bands at the petal bases. Flowers in red, orange or brown are also possible. Dwarf cultivars that grow about 8–12" tall are available. '**Mardi Gras**' is a dwarf cultivar growing to 9" tall. Its masses of star-shaped flowers are striped in mahogany and gold. The foliage of this plant develops bronze-green fall color, usually while the plant is still blooming.

C. tinctoria (this page)

Problems & Pests

Slugs, snails and fungal diseases can be problems. Avoid watering in the evening.

Self-seeding is common with these plants, so they may pop up from year to year in the same area if left to their own devices. Some of the seeds will travel. You may actually find young plants popping up in some very interesting locations.

Corn Cockle
Agrostemma

Height: 24–36" **Spread:** 12" **Flower color:** pink, magenta, purple, white

WHEN I WAS AT A FLOWER MARKET in San Francisco several years ago I saw this very unusual flower. I didn't know anything about it, didn't know how to grow it, but I knew that I really liked it. After finding out it was Corn Cockle, I sowed some of the seed on my hill behind the nursery. I found that it self-sows, but the self-sown flowers were not as vivid as the original plantings. If you want the intense color that these flowers bring to plantings and bouquets, sow seed that you know will give you the result you want.

Planting

Seeding: Direct sow in mid-spring to early summer

Transplanting: February through July

Spacing: 12"

Growing

Corn Cockle prefers **full sun**. It tolerates light shade but with reduced flowering. The soil should be of **poor to average fertility** and **well drained**. Corn Cockle prefers cool temperatures, so don't plant it in heat traps such as against the south or west wall of a house.

Plant Corn Cockle where it will be supported by other plants, because it tends to grow tall and lanky. Twiggy sticks can be inserted in the bed around young plants to support them as they grow.

Corn Cockle plants bloom rapidly from seed. Deadheading extends the blooming period. Although they can self-seed, it is best to sow new seed every year in order to maintain the original color. Left to self-seed, Corn Cockle plants will revert to dark pink.

Tips

Corn Cockle is a tall, loose-growing plant best included in meadow and cottage-style gardens, but it can also be scattered through an informal border to provide occasional bursts of color.

The tiny brownish-black seeds are poisonous when ingested. Make the most of this tall plant at the back of a border, where the seeds will be harder for little hands to reach.

Recommended

A. githago is a fast-growing, willowy plant with white-centered magenta or white flowers. 'Milas' has dark pink flowers. 'Ocean Pearls' has large white flowers. 'Purple Queen'

has gray stems that bear white-centered purple flowers with darker speckles.

Problems & Pests

This plant is generally pest free, though it may have trouble with fungal leaf spot on occasion. To avoid fungal problems, water only in the morning.

Cosmos

Cosmos

Height: 1–7' **Spread:** 12–18" **Flower color:** white, yellow, orange, gold, shades of pink and of red

WHEN I USE COSMOS AS CUT FLOWERS, I take the cuttings as early in the morning as possible, and I make a second cut at the base of the flower stem under warm water. This approach helps preserve the cut flowers for up to two weeks. Plant a few Chocolate Cosmos plants near pathways so you can enjoy the chocolate scent. Friends will think you are making hot fudge or chocolate cookies.

Planting

Seeding: Indoors in late winter; direct sow from mid-March through end of July

Transplanting: After last frost

Spacing: 12–18"

Growing

Cosmos like **full sun.** If not given enough sun, these plants produce weak, floppy stems. The soil should be of **poor or average fertility** and **well drained.** Cosmos are drought tolerant.

C. bipinnatus (this page)

Overfertilizing and overwatering can produce floppy stems and reduce the number of flowers produced. A healthy plant can have a stem of up to $1^1/_2$" in diameter, capable of supporting a plant 3' tall or taller.

Yellow Cosmos does better if sown directly in the garden. Keep faded blooms cut to encourage more buds. Cosmos plants often re-seed.

Cosmos plants are likely to need staking but are difficult to stake. If you want to avoid staking, plant cosmos in a sheltered location or against a fence. You could also grow

shorter varieties. If staking can't be avoided, push twiggy branches into the ground when the plants are young and allow them to grow up between the branches. The branches will be hidden by the mature plants.

Tips

Cosmos are attractive in cottage gardens, at the back of a border or mass planted in an informal bed or border. They combine well with many other tall annuals.

Recommended

C. atrosanguineus (Chocolate Cosmos) has recently become popular among annuals connoisseurs for its fragrant, deep maroon flowers that some claim smell like chocolate. The plant is upright, growing to 30" tall, but tends to flop over a bit when the stems get too long. Although it can be

C. bipinnatus (this page)

treated as a perennial, it looks best if planted from seed each season.

C. bipinnatus (Annual Cosmos) has many cultivars. The flowers come in magenta, rose, pink or white, usually with yellow centers. Old varieties grow 3–6' tall, while some of the newer cultivars grow 12–36" tall. '**Daydream**' grows up to 60" tall and has white flowers flushed with pink at the petal bases. '**Sea Shells**' reaches 42". It bears flowers in many colors, and the petals are rolled into tubes. '**Sensation**' series bears large white or pink flowers on plants up to 4' tall. '**Sonata**' bears red, pink or white flowers on compact plants up to 24" tall.

C. sulphureus (Yellow Cosmos) has gold, orange, scarlet and yellow flowers. Old varieties grow 7' tall, and new varieties grow 1–4' tall. '**Klondike**' is a compact plant about 12–24" tall, with bright yellow or orange-red, single or semi-double flowers. '**Ladybird**' series has compact dwarf plants, 12–14" tall, that rarely need staking. The foliage is not as feathered as it is in other cultivars. '**Polidora**' (Polidor Mix) grows 24–30" tall and is a good choice for long-stemmed cut flowers. Light yellow, gold and bright orange flowers, many bicolored, bloom for an extended period from early summer to frost.

Problems & Pests

Cosmos plants rarely have any problems, but watch for wilt, aster yellows, powdery mildew and aphids.

The name Cosmos *is from the Greek and means 'beautiful.'*

C. atrosanguineus (above), C. bipinnatus (below)

Cut flowers of cosmos make lovely, long-lasting fillers in arrangements.

Creeping Zinnia

Sanvitalia

Height: 4–8"   **Spread:** 15–18"   **Flower color:** yellow or orange; dark brown or black centers

BECAUSE OF ITS COLORFUL SPREADING HABIT, Creeping Zinnia is ideal to use as a groundcover around other drought-tolerant plants. When I installed display gardens in flower shows, I found Creeping Zinnia useful to hide unwanted or ugly spots in the garden. In a hanging basket, this flower combines well with Ivy-leaved Geranium, Sweet Alyssum and Million Bells.

Planting

Seeding: Direct sow in mid-spring

Spacing: 12"

Growing

Creeping Zinnia prefers **full sun**. The soil should be of **average fertility, light, sandy** and **well drained**.

Do not cover the seeds when you sow them because they need light to germinate. Keep them moist until they show their first true leaves. Water sparingly after that.

Tips

Creeping Zinnia can be used as an annual groundcover or edging plant. It is also dramatic in hanging baskets and in mixed containers.

This plant is one of the easiest annuals to grow. It is also one of the easiest to damage with too much care; overwatering and overfertilizing can quickly kill it.

Recommended

S. procumbens forms a low mat of foliage up to 8" tall and spreads its trailing branches 15–18". Black-centered yellow flowers bloom from early summer to fall. 'Sprite' is a mounding plant 8" tall. Its yellow-orange flowers have dark centers. 'Yellow Carpet' is a low-growing plant up to 4" tall and 18" wide. It has bright yellow flowers with dark centers.

Problems & Pests

Keep Creeping Zinnia from getting hit by a sprinkler, or it will suffer mildew and other fungal problems. If you have to water from above, do so in the early morning only so that the plants can dry out before the cool of the evening.

A native of Mexico, Creeping Zinnia produces masses of bright yellow flowers.

The less you do to it, the better your Creeping Zinnia will look.

Cup Flower

Nierembergia

Height: 6–12" **Spread:** 6–12" **Flower color:** blue, purple, white

WHEN I FIRST TRIED TO GROW this particular plant, I didn't have much luck. This was because I was treating it as a shade lover and watering it too much. Once I found that Cup Flower needs good drainage and warm sun, I had no further trouble. It is a winner in hanging baskets and as a border plant along flowerbeds. It should have some shade in the Sacramento Valley and other hot regions of Northern California, but it thrives in full sun otherwise.

Planting

Seeding: Indoors in mid-winter; in mild climates, direct sow in sheltered locations in mid-fall

Transplanting: April; from 4" pots

Spacing: 6–12"

Growing

Cup Flower grows well in **full sun** or **partial shade**. The soil should be **fertile, moist** and **well drained**.

Cup Flower is a perennial used as an annual. It may survive mild winters on the coast, but it is easier to start new plants each year than to protect mature plants over winter.

Tips

Use Cup Flower as a groundcover, for edging beds and borders, and for rock walls, rock gardens, containers and hanging baskets. It grows best when summers are cool, and it can withstand a light frost. Keep this plant out of the hot afternoon sun for best results.

The former species name, hippomanica, *is from the Greek and means 'drives horses crazy.' Whether they went crazy because they loved to eat the plant or from the effects of eating it is unclear.*

Recommended

N. caerulea (*N. hippomanica*) forms a small mound of foliage. This plant bears delicate, cup-shaped flowers in lavender blue with yellow centers. **'Mont Blanc'** has white flowers with yellow centers. **'Purple Robe'** has deep purple flowers with golden eyes and is the hardier of the two cultivars listed here.

Problems & Pests

Slugs, earwigs and snails are likely to be the worst problems for this plant. Because Cup Flower is susceptible to tobacco mosaic virus, don't plant it near any flowering tobacco or tomato plants. If you handle Cup Flower and flowering tobacco or tomato on the same day, wash your hands in buttermilk to avoid spreading the virus.

'Mont Blanc'

Dahlia
Bedding Dahlia
Dahlia

Height: 12–16" **Spread:** 12–18" **Flower color:** purple, pink, white, yellow, orange, red or bicolored

I DON'T KNOW OF ANY ANNUALS MORE DESERVING of attention than dahlias. You can grow these wonderful plants either by sowing the seeds indoors in January in flats for later transplanting or by direct sowing in April. The dazzle of dahlia plants from a pack of seed will reward you not only with color in the garden but with armloads of picking flowers for any occasion. Unlike F1 hybrids, these plants will grow true from seed you can collect yourself.

Planting

Seeding: Indoors in January; direct sow in April

Transplanting: Mid-March through April

Spacing: 12"

Growing

Dahlias prefer **full sun.** The soil should be **fertile, rich in organic matter, moist** and **well drained.** Dahlias are treated as annuals and do very well when purchased as bedding plants from six-packs and discarded at the end of the year. Deadhead to keep the plants blooming and attractive.

All dahlias are tuberous perennials. The tubers of all varieties can be lifted in fall, dried and stored over winter in slightly moist peat moss. Pot them and keep them in a bright room when they start sprouting in mid- to late winter. Divide the tubers by finding the sprouted eye; ensure there is one eye per division.

If you are interested in a particular size, color or form of dahlia, it is best to start it from tubers of that type. You can create your own pre-ferred color scheme by saving your favorite tubers. Seed-grown dahlias vary greatly in color and form because the seed is generally sold in mixed packages. The plants grown from seed in mixed packages are usually 12–14" high.

Tips

Dahlias make attractive, colorful additions to mixed beds and bor-ders and are effective as edging

Andreas Dahl, the Swedish botanist for whom these plants were named, tried to popularize dahlias as a food crop for their edible tubers. They began to receive more attention for their beautiful flowers.

plants. Varieties with unusual or interestingly formed flowers are attractive specimen plants. The adventurous gardener can collect some seedheads in fall and plant those seeds in spring.

Recommended

There are many dahlia hybrids. Most must be grown from tubers, but there are a few that can be started from seed with good results. Examples include *D.* **'Figaro,'** which forms a round, compact plant 12–16" tall. The small, double or semi-double flowers come in a variety of colors, and the plant grows and flowers quickly. It looks good grouped in a

border or in containers. *D.* 'Harlequin' forms compact plants that flower quickly from seed. The flowers are solid or bicolored, single or semi-double in many shades. Many hybrid seeds are sold in mixed packets based on flower shape; for example, semi-cactus, decorative or peony flowered.

Problems & Pests

Dahlias may encounter a few problems: aphids, powdery mildew, slugs and earwigs are the most likely. If a worse problem afflicts your dahlias, it may be best to destroy the infected plants and start over. Gophers enjoy eating the tubers.

Dahlia flowers are categorized by size and by flower type— for example, peony, formal and informal decorative, semi-cactus and waterlily.

Semi-cactus type

Waterlily type

Peony type 'Bishop of Llandaff'

Informal decorative type

Diascia
Twinspur
Diascia

Height: 10–12" **Spread:** 20–24" **Flower color:** varied shades of pink

A HOMEOWNER IN BELVEDERE prided herself on her wonderful garden, and rightfully so. She had a magic touch with plants. When *Diascia* 'Ruby Fields' was brought onto the market, she snatched it up and planted it into a bed with Snapdragon, stocks and delphiniums. It was a great display.

Planting
Seeding: Indoors in spring

Transplanting: March through June; from 4" pots

Spacing: 18"

Growing
Diascia plants prefer **full sun,** but during hot, humid summers they do better in light or partial shade with protection from the afternoon sun. The soil should be **fertile, moist** and **well drained.**

Diascias are generally frost hardy and bloom well into fall. To promote new blooms, cut back stems after flowering. Diascia plants may fade during the hottest part of summer but will revive and produce flowers as temperatures drop in fall.

Tips

Diascia plants are attractive in a rock garden or mass planted in a border. They combine well with Sweet Alyssum, candytufts and other low-growing annuals. Pinch the tips to increase bushiness and flower production.

Recommended

D. barberae is a low-growing plant that bears loose spikes of pink flowers from mid-summer to frost. **'Blackthorn Apricot'** has apricot-colored flowers and flowerheads that point downwards. **'Pink Queen'** has light, shimmery pink flowers on long, slender stalks.

D. **'Coral Belle'** is a quick-growing hybrid that forms a dense mound of bright green foliage. The flowers are a delicate coral pink.

D. **'Ruby Fields'** is a mat-forming hybrid. It produces an abundance of salmon pink flowers for an extended period from late spring to early fall.

D. **'Strawberry Sundae'** is a fairly compact plant with trailing stems and bright pink flowers.

Problems & Pests

Watch out for snails, slugs and in fall, black aphids.

Diascias are perennials grown as annuals in most of California, mainly because these plants do not overwinter well in our heavy soils.

'Strawberry Sundae'

English Daisy

Bellis

Height: 2–8" **Spread:** 2–8" **Flower color:** white, pink, red; yellow centers

I HAVE ALWAYS LOVED THIS WONDERFUL long-blooming annual. The only problem I ever had with it was when it started to re-seed into my dad's manicured lawn. It wasn't long before Dad began pulling and tossing the unwanted visitors. When I complained to my mother, she let me know in no uncertain terms that what Dad considered a weed in his lawn was a weed and I should stay out of it!

Planting

Seeding: Start seed in spring for fall flowering or in fall for spring flowering

Transplanting: Spring or fall

Spacing: 2–8"

Growing

English Daisy grows well in **full sun, partial shade** or **light shade**. The soil should be of **average to high fertility, cool, moist** and **humus rich**.

English Daisy is the easiest plant to grow from transplants.

Tips

English Daisy is a real workhorse in the garden. Use it on rock walls, in open woodland gardens, planters and borders. It can also be used as a groundcover.

English Daisy has a habit of self-seeding and may show up where you least expect it, including in your lawn. It adapts very well in low-maintenance lawns. Deadheading to control spread is possible but decidedly time-consuming because English Daisy is low growing. If immaculate lawns are required, place this plant in beds well away from lawns and consider taking the time to deadhead.

Recommended

B. perennis is a low, spreading perennial grown here as an annual because it tends to look ratty after two or three seasons. Yellow-centered white, pink or red flowers bloom from mid-spring to late summer. '**Dresden China**' is a small, compact plant with light pink double flowers. '**Habanero**' has pink, white or red flowers that have long petals. '**Pomponette**' has pink, red or white flowers with quilled petals. '**White Pearl**' has white double flowers.

Problems & Pests

Fungal leaf spots and aphids are possible, but not serious, problems. Watering only in the morning will avoid most problems.

Flowering Maple
Chinese Lantern
Abutilon

Height: 4' **Spread:** 2–4' **Flower color:** white, red, pink, yellow, orange

FLOWERING MAPLE can be grown as an annual, perennial or shrub. In poorly drained soils, which is the case in much of Northern California, this plant can rot during winter so is grown as an annual. However, in San Francisco, Flowering Maple specimens become beautiful, yet leggy, trees because of the sandy, well-drained soil and the mild winter temperatures. Flowering Maple is at its best when started fresh every spring from seeds or cuttings.

Planting

Seeding: Sow indoors or direct sow in spring; soil temperature 60° F

Transplanting: April to May

Spacing: 24"

Growing

Flowering Maple likes **full sun** and **well-drained, moderately fertile** soil. Ensure you provide adequate water.

Some sources claim that Flowering Maple will flower better if allowed to become root-bound in its container. If you do let it become root-bound, make sure you provide the extra watering the plant will need. Pinch the tips of the stems to encourage bushier growth.

Propagate by seed or by softwood cuttings in spring, or by semi-hardwood cuttings in mid- to late summer. Seeds gathered from local plants are often sterile.

Flowering Maple is not related to maples (genus Acer*), but the foliage has a maple-leaf shape.*

Tips

Flowering Maple is a large shrub or small tree in its native South America and is grown as an annual here. It is grown mainly for its attractive flowers and should be planted where the blooms can be appreciated.

Use Flowering Maple as a specimen or container plant or in beds. The plant can be trained as a standard or as informal espalier. As a houseplant it can be moved outdoors in the summer and back into the house in winter.

As an annual it combines well with Hollyhock, delphiniums and other tall annuals. It likes shade in the hot spots of the Sacramento Valley, full sun along the coast and morning sun in other parts of Northern California.

Flowering Maple will attract hummingbirds and butterflies to your garden.

Recommended

A. hybridum is a catchall group comprising hybrids of various *Abutilon* species. The plants have upright, arching growth and white, yellow, orange or red flowers in spring. Cultivars with white and yellow flowers bloom for the whole summer. Many cultivars are available; the following are some of the most popular. As annuals they generally reach a height of 4' and spread 2–4' but may grow larger depending on your garden. '**Kentish Belle**' has yellow-orange blooms. '**Moonchimes**' is a more compact plant that produces large yellow flowers from spring to fall. '**Souvenir de Bonn**' has variegated foliage. This cultivar produces pale orange blooms with darker orange to red veins continuously from spring to fall.

Problems & Pests

Flowering Maple may suffer attacks by aphids, caterpillars, flea beetles, scale, whiteflies, rust, mosaic virus and some fungal leaf spot. In fall and winter, watch out for slugs and snails.

To create a more vertical tree-like structure, allow only one main stem to remain and remove all side shoots from it until it reaches the desired height. Then pinch the main tip to force lateral bushiness at the top of the plant.

Flowering Tobacco
Nicotiana

Height: 1–5' **Spread:** 10–18" **Flower color:** red, pink, green, white, purple

FOR STRIKING FLOWERS IN THE GARDEN, nothing matches the lovely flowering tobaccos. My finest hour with flowering tobacco plants was when I featured them in my garden at the Alameda County Fair. I had raised the plants at a modest garden temperature of 65 to 80°. The temperature at the fair in Pleasanton was 125° in the shade—quite a difference. By mid-afternoon the plants looked very tired, and I was worried that they might die. I applied foliar feeding that evening. When I checked them the next morning, they were as wonderful as the morning I had planted them. I averted what would have been a disaster of having the plants in my show succumb to the heat.

Nicotiana *was named for Jean Nicot (1530–1600), a French consul in Portugal. He is credited with introducing this plant to France.*

Planting

Seeding: Indoors in early spring; direct sow later

Transplanting: In spring once soil has warmed; from six-packs and 4" pots

Spacing: 8–12"

Growing

Flowering tobaccos grow equally well in **full sun** or **light or partial shade.** The soil should be **fertile,** high in **organic matter, moist** and **well drained.**

The seeds require light for germination, so leave them uncovered.

Tips

Flowering tobaccos are popular in beds and borders. The dwarf varieties do well in containers. *N. alata* combines well with low-growing zinnias and other colorful annuals. *N. sylvestris* is a wonderful plant

N. sylvestris (above), *N. alata* (below)

N. *alata* (this page)

to combine with dahlias and other tall annuals such as Hollyhock. Staking is rarely required for flowering tobacco plants, even for the tall selections.

Do not eat these plants. All parts are **poisonous** if eaten.

Do not place these plants near tomatoes because they are members of the same plant family and share many of the same diseases. The flowering tobacco may attract and harbor diseases, including the tomato hornworm, which will hardly affect the flowering tobacco but that can kill tomatoes.

Recommended

N. *alata* is an upright plant that grows up to 5' tall and has a strong, sweet fragrance. '**Merlin**' series has dwarf plants ideal for mixed planters. Its flowers may be red,

pink, purple, white or pale green on plants 10–15" tall. 'Nicki' series has many colored, fragrant blooms that stay open all day. The compact plants grow up to 18" tall. 'Sensation' grows up to 30" tall and bears red, white or pink flowers that stay open all day.

N. sylvestris grows up to 4' tall and bears white blooms that give off a wonderful scent in the evening.

N. sylvestris (above)

Problems & Pests

Tobacco mosaic virus, aphids and downy or powdery mildew may cause occasional problems. Budworm is the worst enemy of this particular plant.

Flowering tobaccos were originally cultivated for the wonderful scent of the flowers. At first, the flowers were available only in a greenish color and they opened only in the evening and at night. In attempts to expand the variety of colors and keep the flowers open during the day, the popular scent has, in some cases, been lost.

Photo (right) showing *N. sylvestris* (top), *N. alata* (bottom), planted with *Cleome* (left)

Forget-Me-Not
Myosotis

Height: 6–12 " **Spread:** 6 " or wider **Flower color:** blue, pink, white

FORGET-ME-NOT is easier to grow than its cousin Chinese Forget-me-not, which requires full sun. Forget-me-not requires shade and moisture to be happy. It dies out completely when the valley temperature soars to over 95° F but is quite content in coastal areas where it survives some heat as long as evening temperatures drop as the fog comes in. It has become naturalized in many areas of California along streambeds. I use it as a colorful groundcover in my *Cymbidium* orchid bed.

Planting
Seeding: Direct sow in fall or early spring

Spacing: 8"

The common name refers to the way this plant lives a short life after blooming but then reappears as new seedlings all over the garden.

Growing

Forget-me-not prefers **light or partial shade** but tolerates full sun if the weather isn't too hot. The soil should be **fertile, moist** and **well drained.** Adding lots of **organic matter** to the soil will help it retain moisture while maintaining good drainage.

Seeds sown in fall will flower in early spring, and seeds sown in spring will flower in summer or fall. This flower self-seeds easily. Once you allow Forget-me-not to go to seed, you will have it everywhere. But you'll love it.

Tips

Forget-me-not is a short-lived perennial that is treated as an annual. It can be used in the front of flowerbeds or to edge beds and borders, in mixed containers and in rock gardens and on rock walls. You can also mix it with naturalized spring-flowering bulbs. Forget-me-not thrives in cooler parts of the garden. In the Sacramento Valley and other hot summer climates, it should be treated as a winter-blooming plant.

Recommended

M. sylvatica forms a low mound of basal leaves. Clusters of small blue or white flowers with yellow centers are held on narrow, fuzzy stems above the foliage. 'Ball' series has compact plants with flowers in several colors.

Problems & Pests

Slugs and snails, downy mildew, powdery mildew and rust may cause occasional trouble. Water in the morning to avoid pest and disease problems.

Forget-me-not is a delightful addition to woodland or wet areas and wildflower gardens.

Fried-Egg Flower
Meadow Foam, Poached Egg Plant
Limnanthes

Height: 4–12" **Spread**: 6–18" **Flower color:** bicolored yellow and white

THIS IS ANOTHER IDEAL PLANT, along with Forget-me-not, for wet spots in the garden. It can also be successfully used under hydrangeas during winter to bring some brighter color to the garden. Early-summer watering will keep this plant blooming into June.

Planting

Seeding: Direct sow in mid-spring

Transplanting: January to February, so winter rains can water the plants

Spacing: 6–12"

Growing

Fried-egg Flower grows well in **full sun** but benefits from a bit of afternoon shade. The soil should be **average to fertile, moist** and **well drained**. It tolerates swamp conditions in cool weather but should be allowed to follow the California weather pattern and dry out in summer.

This plant is best sown directly because it resents having its roots disturbed. If you want to start it early indoors, use peat pellets or pots or plant the seeds in one-gallon plastic containers so the plants can be placed directly into the garden without any root disturbance.

Tips

This attractive plant can be included at the edge of a border or path, in a rock garden or in a mixed container. The flowers attract bees to the garden, so you may wish to avoid planting Fried-egg Flower near a patio or children's play area.

Recommended

L. douglasii can be upright, but it is usually a fairly dense, spreading plant. It bears yellow-centered white flowers that look like sunny-side–up eggs.

Problems & Pests

Fried-egg Flower rarely suffers from any problems.

The genus name, Limnanthes, *is derived from the Greek words* limne *(a marsh) and* anthos *(a flower), describing the natural habitat of the genus.*

Geranium
Pelargonium

Height: 8–24" **Spread**: 5"–4' **Flower color**: red, pink, lilac, orange, salmon, white, purple

THESE WONDERFUL PLANTS have been used in the center roadway strips in San Francisco, where they are real showstoppers with all the blooms coming on at once before fading. The plants are watered only once a week, and because of the cool weather tempered by the heat from the traffic, they have done wonderfully. The high volume of traffic gets in the way of the low-flowing moths that would lay their eggs on the plants and become budworms. Unfortunately the plants are **not** deadheaded sufficiently to keep them at their best. They seem to forgive all of this and come into bloom again.

Planting

Seeding: Indoors in early winter; direct sow in spring

Transplanting: Early March to fall; from 4" pots

Spacing: Ivy-leaved Geranium, 24–36"; Zonal Geranium, about 12"

Growing

Geraniums prefer **full sun** but tolerate partial shade, although they may not bloom as profusely. The soil should be **fertile** and **well drained**. Keep the plants well watered but allow them to dry out between waterings. If they wilt, they will recover.

It is easy and economical to have a good show of geraniums if you plant from 4" pots. However, if you would like to try starting your own from seed, start them indoors in early winter and cover them with clear plastic to maintain humidity until they germinate. Once the

P. peltatum (this page)

P. peltatum (this page)

seedlings have three or four leaves, transplant them into individual 3–4" pots. Keep them in bright locations because they need lots of light to maintain their compact shape. To prevent damping off, spread peat moss on the surface of the seedbed.

Deadheading is essential to keep geraniums blooming and looking neat. The flowerheads are attached to long stems that break off easily where they attach to the plant. Some gardeners prefer to snip off just the flowering end of this stem in order to avoid damaging the plant.

Tips

Geraniums are perennials that are very popular grown as annuals. Ivy-leaved Geranium is most often used in hanging baskets and containers to take advantage of its trailing habit, but it is also interesting when used as a bedding plant to form a bushy, spreading groundcover. Zonal Geranium can be used in beds, borders and containers.

Recommended

The following species and varieties are some of the easier ones to start from seed. Many popular varieties can be propagated only from cuttings and must be purchased as plants. To be sure to get the plant you want, purchase it in bloom in 4" pots. The varieties are astounding and defy all attempts to simplify the nomenclature.

P. peltatum (Ivy-leaved Geranium) grows up to 12" tall and up to 4' wide. A wide range of colors is available. **'Summer Showers'** series, one of the first seed mixtures that became available for Ivy-leaved Geranium, can take four or more months to flower from seed. 'Tornado' series is very good for hanging baskets and containers. The plants are quite compact, and the flowers are either lilac or white.

P. zonale (P. x *hortorum)* (Zonal Geranium) grows up to 24" tall and 12" wide. Dwarf varieties grow up to 8" tall and 5" wide. The flowers are red, pink, purple, orange or white. 'Orbit' series has attractive, early-blooming, compact plants, with different flower colors generally sold in a mixed packet. Some individual colors are available. 'Pinto' series is available in all colors, and seed is generally sold by the color.

Problems & Pests

Aphids will flock to overfertilized plants but can usually be washed off before they do much damage. Leaf spot, rust and blight may bother geraniums in cool, moist soil.

Edema is an unusual condition to which geraniums are susceptible if overwatered. The leaf cells burst, and a warty surface develops on the leaves. There is no cure, although it can be avoided through careful, regular watering; e.g. every three days, and by removing any damaged leaves as the plant grows. The condition is more common in Ivy-leaved Geranium.

Ivy-leaved Geranium is one of the most beautiful plants to include in a mixed hanging basket.

P. zonale (this page)

Globe Amaranth
Gomphrena

Height: 6–30" **Spread:** 6–12"
Flower color: purple, pink, white, sometimes red

GLOBE AMARANTHS can be added to any flower arrangement to accent other plants. The flowers of a globe amaranth are perfect in dried arrangements. The plants love to be crowded into small pots and small areas of the garden. Crowding these plants makes a wonderful, living, everblooming bouquet.

Planting

Seeding: Indoors in late winter

Transplanting: Mid-March through mid-June

Spacing: 10"

Globe amaranth flowers are popular for cutting and drying because they keep their color and form well when dried. Pick the flowers before they are completely open and dry them upside down in a cool, dry location.

Growing

Globe amaranth plants prefer **full sun** and like hot weather. The soil should be of **average fertility** and **well drained**.

Seeds will germinate more quickly if soaked for two to four days before sowing. They need warm soil (above 70° F) to sprout.

Tips

Use globe amaranths in an informal or cottage garden. These plants are often underused because they don't start flowering until later in summer than many other annuals. Don't overlook them; they are worth the wait and provide color from mid-summer until the first frost. The plants respond well to a moderate feeding of compost or chicken manure during the growing season.

Recommended

G. globosa forms a rounded, bushy plant growing to 24" tall and 12" wide. It is dotted with clover-like flowers with pink, purple or white bracts, which make up the showy part of the flowerhead. '**Buddy**' has more compact plants, 6–12" tall, with deep purple flowers. '**Lavender Lady**' becomes a larger plant, up to 30" tall, and bears lavender purple flowers.

G. '**Strawberry Fields**' is a hybrid with bright orange-red flowerheads. It grows about 30" tall and spreads about half as much.

Problems & Pests

Globe amaranth plants are susceptible to some fungal diseases, such as gray mold and leaf spot. To avoid such problems, water only in the morning and ensure that the soil is well drained.

Godetia
Clarkia, Satin Flower
Clarkia (Godetia)

Height: 12–36" **Spread:** 10–12" **Flower color:** pink, red, purple, white; some bicolored

THE BLOOMS OF GODETIAS, with a texture that looks like tissue paper, are outstanding in any annual bed. I have also seen wonderful displays of these flowers in moss baskets. They bloom all summer along the coastal areas of Northern California and are at their best in early spring in warmer climates such as the Sacramento Valley.

Planting
Seeding: Direct sow in spring or late summer

Transplanting: March through July; from six-packs or 4" pots

Spacing: 6–8"

The genus name, Clarkia, *honors William Clark of the famed Lewis and Clark expedition.*

Growing

Godetias grow equally well in **full sun** or **light shade**. The soil should be **well drained, light, sandy** and of **poor or average fertility**. These plants don't like to be overwatered, so be sure to let them dry out between waterings. They do well in cool weather.

Direct sow seeds in spring for summer bloom and in mid- to late summer for fall bloom. Starting seeds indoors is difficult and not recommended.

Tips

Godetias are useful in beds, borders, containers and rock gardens. The flowers can be used for fresh arrangements.

Recommended

C. amoena (*Godetia amoena, G. grandiflora*) (Godetia, Satin Flower) is a bushy, upright plant, 30" tall and 12" wide. It bears clusters of ruffled, cup-shaped flowers in shades of pink, red, white and purple. '**Satin**' series has compact plants that grow 8–12" tall. The single flowers come in many colors, including some bicolors.

C. concinna (Red Ribbons) is a California native often found in wildflower mixes. It grows 18" tall and 12" wide and bears pinkish purple flowers. It is best used on hillsides and areas that receive infrequent watering.

C. unguiculata (*C. elegans*) (Clarkia, Rocky Mountain Garland Flower) is a tall, branching plant that grows 12–36" tall and spreads up to 10".

C. amoena (this page)

Its small ruffled flowers can be pink, purple, red or white. '**Apple Blossom**' bears apricot-pink double flowers. '**Royal Bouquet**' bears very ruffled double flowers in pink, red or light purple.

Problems & Pests

Root rot can afflict godetias in poorly drained soil.

Heliotrope
Cherry Pie Plant
Heliotropium

Height: 8–24"   **Spread:** 12–24"   **Flower color:** purple, occasionally white

THE WONDERFUL FRAGRANCE OF THE HELIOTROPE in the gardens of Harmony Hill are described by Joan Hockaday in her book *The Gardens of San Francisco*. I interviewed the owner of the garden on several occasions, and after each interview I felt an everlasting love for this easy-to-grow annual. It is a wonderful addition to seaside gardens and thrives in the Sacramento Valley if given a break from the hot afternoon sun.

Heliotrope can be grown indoors as a houseplant in a sunny window.

Planting

Seeding: Indoors in mid-winter
Transplanting: March to early April
Spacing: 12–18"

Growing

Heliotrope grows best in **full sun.** The soil should be **fertile,** rich in **organic matter, moist** and **well drained.**

Although the species is listed as a perennial, it rarely overwinters outdoors. It does not tolerate cold and wet.

Tips

This plant is ideal for growing near windows and patios, where the wonderful scent of the flowers can be enjoyed. Plants that are a little underwatered tend to have a stronger scent.

Heliotrope can be pinched and shaped into a tree form by pinching off the lower branches until it reaches the desired height and then pinching the top to encourage the plant to bush out. Create a shorter, bushy form by pinching all the tips that develop.

Recommended

H. arborescens grows 18–24" tall with an equal spread and produces large clusters of scented, purple flowers all summer. Some new cultivars are not as strongly scented as the species. '**Blue Wonder**' is a compact plant, growing up to 16" tall, which was bred to have heavily scented flowers. It bears dark purple flowers. '**Dwarf Marine**' ('Mini Marine') is a compact, bushy plant, 8–12" tall, with fragrant purple flowers. It makes a good houseplant for a bright location. '**Marine**' has violet blue flowers and grows about 18" tall.

Problems & Pests

Aphids and whiteflies can be problems.

This old-fashioned flower has become very popular—no surprise considering its attractive foliage, flowers and scent.

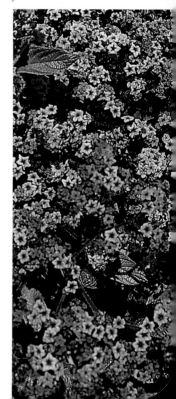

Hollyhock
Alcea

Height: 5–8' **Spread:** 24"
Flower color: yellow, white, apricot, pink,
red, purple, reddish black

HOLLYHOCK was originally introduced
into California by the Padres of the
California Missions. One of the best uses
of this plant, with its spires of pastel colors,
is in the back of a garden. I have, however,
seen it planted somewhat randomly in
well-kept, established landscapes. The
effect is quite unusual and very dramatic
in that the varying heights in the garden
add a colorful dimension. Hollyhock combines well with other tall annuals such as
Spider Flower and Sunflower.

Planting

Seeding: Indoors in early winter or direct
sow mid-March through April

Transplanting: After last frost

Spacing: 12"

Growing

Hollyhock prefers **full sun** but tolerates partial shade. The soil should be of **average to
rich fertility** and **well drained**. Ensure the
plant receives adequate water, especially
when the weather is hot and dry.

In a windy location Hollyhock plants will
need to be staked. Planting against a fence
or wall will give some support. A Hollyhock
plant will be shorter and bushier with
smaller flower spikes if the main stem is
pinched out early in the season. Several
shorter flower stems will then develop,
which are less likely to be broken by the
wind and can be left unstaked.

Tips

Because it is so tall, Hollyhock looks best at the back of the border or in the center of an island bed.

Plant Hollyhock in a different part of the garden each year to keep rust disease at bay. Old-fashioned Hollyhock types typically bear single flowers, grow much taller than newer hybrids and resist disease better.

Recommended

A. rosea forms a rosette of basal leaves; the tall stalk that develops bears ruffled single or double blooms. 'Chater's Double' bears double flowers in a wide range of colors. 'Nigra' bears reddish black single flowers with yellow centers. 'Summer Carnival' bears double flowers in yellows and reds. It blooms in early summer and produces flowers lower on the stem than other cultivars.

Problems & Pests

Hollyhock rust is the biggest problem. This plant is also susceptible to bacterial and fungal leaf spot. Slugs and cutworms occasionally attack young growth. Mallow flea beetles, aphids and Japanese beetles may cause trouble. Do not plant Hollyhock near Snapdragon, Begonia or roses.

Hollyhock was originally grown as a food plant. The leaves were added to salads.

Impatiens
Impatiens

Height: 6–36" **Spread**: 12–24" **Flower color**: shades of purple, red, pink, orange, white or bicolored

I DON'T BELIEVE THERE IS A MORE REWARDING ANNUAL than an impatiens. In the fall these plants set an abundance of seed that looks like caterpillars. When he was quite young, my son, Bill, pointed out that the impatiens plants I was selling in the nursery were full of worms. We showed him what the seedpods looked like and how they opened when touched. At Thanksgiving, my grandchildren would find the Busy Lizzie Impatiens plants that were loaded with seedpods and squeal with delight as the pods exploded in their hands.

Planting

Seeding: Indoors in mid-winter; Balsam Impatiens indoors in late winter

Transplanting: Early March, once soil has warmed, through summer

Spacing: 12–18"

Growing

All impatiens do best in **partial shade.** They grow well in full sun in coastal areas and tolerate full shade in the Sacramento Valley and other hot spots in Northern California. New Guinea and Balsam Impatiens are better adapted to sunny locations than Busy Lizzie is. The soil should be **fertile, humus rich, moist** and **well drained.**

When seeding, don't cover seeds—they germinate best when exposed to light. Do not allow the soil to dry out as the seeds sprout.

I. walleriana (this page)

Tips

Busy Lizzie is known for its ability to grow and flower profusely in even the deepest shade. It requires full sun along Northern California coastal regions but should be kept in shade elsewhere. Mass plant Busy Lizzie in beds under trees, along fences or

I. balsamina (above), New Guinea (below)

walls that create shade, in porch planters or in hanging baskets.

New Guinea Impatiens is almost shrubby and is popular in patio planters, beds and borders. It grows well in full sun and may not flower as profusely in deep shade. This plant is grown as much for its variegated leaves as for its flowers.

Balsam Impatiens was popular in the Victorian era and is experiencing a revival in popularity. It has an upright habit and is attractive grouped in beds and borders.

Poor Man's Rhododendron can be used as a shrub in frost-free areas of the Bay Area. In the warmer interior valleys, it needs shade or morning-only sun.

Recommended

New varieties of impatiens are introduced every year, expanding the selection of size, form and color. The following are a few that are popular year after year.

I. balsamina (Balsam Impatiens) grows 12–36" tall and up to 18" wide. The flowers come in shades of purple, red, pink or white. Several double-flowered cultivars are available, such as **'Camellia-flowered,'** with pink, red or white flowers on plants up to 24" tall; **'Tom Thumb,'** with pink, red, purple or white flowers on compact plants to 12" tall; or **'Topknot,'** with large flowers in shades of pink held above the dense foliage on plants 12" tall.

I. **New Guinea Group** (New Guinea Impatiens) plants grow 12–24" tall and spread 12" or more. The flowers come in shades of red, orange, pink, purple or white. The foliage is often variegated with a yellow stripe down the center of each leaf. 'Tango' is the most common variety to grow from seed. The plants grow 12–18" tall and wide and have orange flowers.

I. sodenii (Poor Man's Rhododendron) is a large perennial in its native tropical Africa and is grown as a shade-loving annual in the interior valleys of Northern California. It produces an abundance of lilac purple to pink flowers in summer. It attains a height and spread of 3'. Along the coast and in the Bay Area, where the temperature does not fall below 36° F, this plant is an ever-blooming perennial that reaches heights of 8–10' with an equal or slightly greater spread.

I. walleriana (Busy Lizzie) grows 6–18" tall and up to 24" wide. The flowers come in shades of red, orange, pink, purple, white or bicolor. 'Accent' grows 10" tall, 12–18" wide and bears flowers in a wide range of colors; some flowers have a white star pattern on the petals. 'Elfin' series is a common group of cultivars. The flowers are available in many shades, including bicolors. The plants grow about 12" tall but may spread more widely. 'Mosaic' has uniquely colored flowers; the margins and most of the petals are speckled in a darker shade of the petal color. 'Tempo' features a wide range of colors, including bicolors and flowers with contrasting margins on the petals. 'Victoria Rose' is an award-winning cultivar that has deep pink double or semi-double flowers.

New Guinea (this page)

The name Impatiens refers to the impatient nature of the seedpods. When ripe, the seedpods burst open with the slightest touch and scatter their seeds.

Larkspur
Annual Delphinium
Consolida (Delphinium)

Height: 12–36" **Spread:** 6–14" **Flower color:** blue, purple, pink, white

LARKSPUR IS AN IDEAL companion plant to Sunflower, Hollyhock and other tall annuals and is an excellent cut flower for large bouquets. Larkspur is heat tolerant in the Sacramento Valley. I think another common name for this plant should be Snail Food, as snails seem to really enjoy eating it.

Planting
Seeding: Indoors in mid-winter; direct sow in early or mid-spring
Transplanting: Late March through April; from six-packs or 4" pots
Spacing: 12"

Growing

Larkspur does equally well in **full sun** or **light shade**. The soil should be **fertile**, rich in **organic matter** and **well drained**. Keep the roots of the plants cool and add a light mulch—dried grass clippings or shredded leaves work well. Don't mulch too closely to the base of the plant or it may develop crown rot.

Seeds started indoors may benefit from being chilled in the refrigerator for one week prior to sowing. When transplanting from six-packs, score the roots so they will spread.

Deadheading will keep these plants blooming well into fall.

'Dwarf Rocket'

These flowers look good at the back of a border and make excellent cut flowers for arrangements.

Tips

Plant groups of Larkspur in mixed borders or cottage gardens. The tallest varieties may require staking to stay upright.

Recommended

C. ajacis (C. ambigua, Delphinium ajacis) is an upright plant with feathery foliage and spikes of purple, blue, pink or white flowers. **'Dwarf Rocket'** series includes plants that grow 12–20" tall and 6–10" wide, with blooms in many colors. **'Giant Imperial'** series also comes in many colors. The plants grow 24–36" tall and up to 14" wide.

Problems & Pests

Slugs and snails are troublemakers. Powdery mildew and crown or root rot are avoidable if you water thoroughly but not too often, and in the morning only. Make sure the plants have good air circulation.

Lobelia
Edging Lobelia
Lobelia

Height: 3–6" **Spread:** 3–18" or more **Flower color:** purple, blue, pink, white, red

LOBELIA is one of the best blue-flowering plants. Along the coast it grows all year long. It can take frost down to 28° F with only a slight amount of damage to the foliage. A floating row cover will protect the plants to even colder temperatures. In the Sacramento Valley, where the temperature can climb to over 110° F, I have seen Lobelia doing very well in moss baskets hanging from the branches of trees that provide it with adequate shade.

Planting

Seeding: Indoors in mid-winter

Transplanting: March to August

Spacing: 6"

Growing

Lobelia grows well in **full sun** or **partial shade.** The soil should be **fertile,** high in **organic matter, moist** and **fairly well drained.** Lobelia likes cool summer nights. It tolerates the heat in the hot valley areas provided it gets adequate water and afternoon shade.

Lobelia seedlings are prone to damping off. See the 'Starting Annuals from Seed' section in the Introduction for information on proper propagation techniques to help avoid damping off.

'Cascade' (above), 'Sapphire' (below)

Tips

Use Lobelia along the edges of beds and borders, on rock walls, in rock gardens, mixed containers or hanging baskets. It combines well with many tall annuals.

You can trim Lobelia back after the first wave of flowers, but it really doesn't recover from shearing back. It is best to replace old with new plants. Lobelia may stop blooming in the hottest part of summer but will usually bounce back in fall. It may wilt during hot days but will recover overnight.

Recommended

L. erinus may be rounded and bushy or low and trailing. The species bears flowers in shades of blue, purple, red, pink or white. **'Cambridge Blue'** is a compact plant bearing powder blue flowers and light green leaves. **'Cascade'** series is a trailing form with flowers in many shades. **'Crystal Palace'** is a compact plant that rarely grows more than 4" tall. This cultivar has dark, bronzy green foliage and dark blue flowers. **'Sapphire'** has white-centered blue flowers on trailing plants.

Problems & Pests

Rust, leaf spot and slugs may be troublesome.

Love-in-a-mist
Devil-in-a-Bush, Wild Fennel
Nigella

Height: 16–24" **Spread:** 9–12" **Flower color:** blue, white, pink, purple

THIS IS ONE OF THE MOST SPECTACULAR and useful cutting flowers I can imagine. My first introduction to this plant was when my dad gave my mom a bouquet that contained some Love-in-a-mist seedpods. When the flowers faded, my grandmother collected the seed from the seedpods and planted them, so we were able to enjoy the Love-in-a-mist for a while longer.

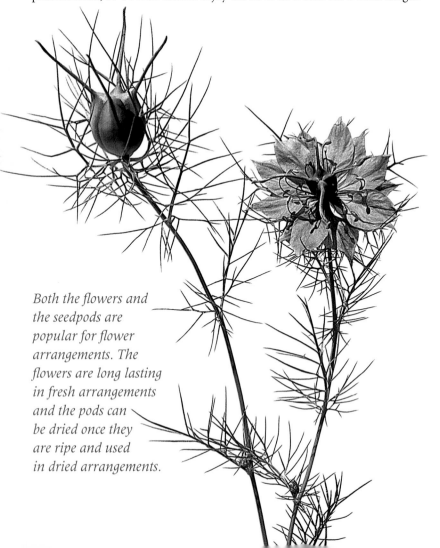

Both the flowers and the seedpods are popular for flower arrangements. The flowers are long lasting in fresh arrangements and the pods can be dried once they are ripe and used in dried arrangements.

Planting

Seeding: Direct sow around last frost date; indoors in late winter

Transplanting: March; from 4" pots

Spacing: 10–15"

Growing

Love-in-a-mist prefers **full sun to partial shade.** The soil should be of **average fertility, moist, light** and **well drained.**

This plant has a long taproot and resents being transplanted, so it is best to direct sow. Sowing at two-week intervals all spring will prolong the blooming period. If starting indoors, use peat pots or pellets to avoid damaging the roots when the plant is put in the garden. Love-in-a-mist plants have a tendency to self-sow and may show up in unexpected spots in your garden for years to come.

Tips

This attractive, airy plant is used in mixed beds and borders where the flowers appear to be floating over the delicate foliage. The blooming may slow down and the plants may die back if the weather gets too hot. In the hot interior valleys the plants will dry up but not before they set the wonderful seedpods.

The stems can be a bit floppy and may benefit from being staked with twiggy branches. Poke the branches around the plants while they are young, and the plants will grow up between the twigs. If a plant flops over, just cut it back. The new growth will be more sturdy.

Recommended

N. damascena forms a loose mound of finely divided foliage. It grows 18–24" tall and spreads about half this much. The light blue flowers darken as they mature. '**Miss Jekyll**' series bears semi-double flowers in rose pink, sky blue or deep cornflower blue that pairs especially well with golden yellow coreopsis. The plants grow to about 18" in height. '**Mulberry Rose**' bears light pink flowers that mature to dark pink. '**Persian Jewel**' series is one of the most common cultivars. Plants in this series usually grow to 16" tall and have flowers in many colors.

Lychnis
Crown Pink, Maltese Cross
Lychnis

Height: 24"–4' **Spread:** 12–18" **Flower color:** magenta, white, scarlet, red

IN NORTHERN CALIFORNIA GARDENS, many common names float around from plant to plant, a practice that leads to unfortunate confusion. *Lychnis coronaria* is sold here as Maltese Cross, as is *Lychnis chalcedonica*, even though they are distinctly different species. In most areas *L. coronaria* is known as Crown Pink. To add to the confusion, *L. coronaria* is also known as Dusty Miller, Mullein Pink and Rose Campion. Regardless of what it's called, the wonderful gray foliage of *L. coronaria* will provide a nice accent to any bed of annual flowers.

Planting

Seeding: Direct sow in late spring; soil temperature 68–70° F

Transplanting: After risk of frost

Spacing: 12–18"

Growing

Lychnis plants grow equally well in **full sun** or **partial shade**. The soil should be of **average fertility, moist** and **well drained**.

These plants are quite short-lived. They do tend to self-seed, though, and will repopulate the garden with new plants as old ones die out. They re-seed easily in gravel pathways, from where young plants can be easily transplanted. They tolerate oak root fungus.

Lychnis plants can be propagated by basal cuttings. Division can be done in spring, though these short-lived plants may not need it.

L. chalcedonica (above), *L. coronaria* (below)

Deadhead the flowers to extend the bloom period and to keep the plants from re-seeding throughout the garden.

Tips

Lychnis specimens are beautiful, carefree additions to a border, cottage garden or naturalized garden.

The tall plants may need some support, particularly if they are in a windy location. Peony supports or twiggy branches pushed into the soil before the plants get too tall are best and are less noticeable than having the plants tied to stakes.

If the plants get leggy, it is an indication that they are getting too much water. Correct this by cutting back the main flower stems and allowing the plants to re-bloom.

L. coronaria (both pages)

Recommended

L. chalcedonica (Maltese Cross) is a stiff, upright plant. It grows 36–48" tall and 12–18" wide. The scarlet flowers are borne in clusters in early and mid-summer. Some support may be required to keep this plant standing upright. 'Alba' has white flowers.

L. coronaria (Crown Pink, Maltese Cross) is a perennial grown as an annual. It forms an upright mass of silvery gray leaves and branching stems. It grows 24–36" tall and about 18" wide. The plant is dotted in late summer with magenta pink flowers, which are very striking against the silvery foliage. 'Alba' has white flowers. 'Angel's Blush' has white flowers with reddish pink centers. 'Atrosanguinea' has red flowers. *L. coronaria* also self-seeds more readily and can take drier conditions than *L. chalcedonica*.

Roots from all plants in the Lychnis *family contain saponin, which produces a soapy foam when stirred in water.*

Mallow
Lavatera

Height: 2–8' **Spread:** 3–6' **Flower color:** pink, red, white

MALLOWS ARE PERFECT for Northern California gardeners who want an immediate backdrop for their vegetable gardens. A mallow plant makes a great temporary hedge as it grows three to six feet in one season, even where the soil isn't the best. With sufficient drainage, sun and water, these plants produce a profusion of flowers. In most areas mallows are best used as early-spring-flowering annuals. In the hot interior valleys, the plants may get stressed in full sun, but will tolerate the heat if given afternoon shade. To ensure lots of blooms, keep the old blooms groomed.

Planting

Seeding: Indoors in late winter; direct sow in spring

Transplanting: Mid-March through July; from 4" pots or one-gallon containers

Spacing: 18–24"

Growing

Mallows prefer **full sun**. The soil should be of **average fertility, light** and **well drained**. These plants like cool, moist weather but tolerate heat if given sufficient water and if protected from wind exposure. In coastal areas they are surprisingly resistant to wind.

Mallow plants resent having their roots disturbed when they are transplanted and tend to do better when planted directly in the garden. If starting seeds indoors, use 4" pots or peat pots.

Tips

Mallows can be used in a variety of ways. In a bed or border they can be used to provide a colorful backdrop behind smaller plants. Along a property line or driveway, they can be used as temporary hedges. Mallow plants grow to be fairly large and shrubby and mix well in shrub beds. The flowers can be used for cutting.

Though there are only 25 species of Lavatera, *they are a diverse group containing annuals, biennials, perennials and shrubs.*

'Silver Cup' (above), 'Mont Blanc' (below)

Recommended

L. trimestris is large and bushy, growing up to 3–6' tall with an equal spread. This plant bears red, pink or white funnel-shaped flowers from mid-summer to fall. **'Beauty'** series is compact, growing to 24", and bears flowers in a variety of colors. **'Mont Blanc'** bears white flowers on compact plants that grow about 24–36" tall. **'Silver Cup'** has cup-shaped light pink flowers with dark pink veins. It also grows 24–36" tall.

Alternate Species

The following plants work well when grown as annuals. If you wish to overwinter them, apply a 4" mulch in fall. This will protect the roots sufficiently to promote regrowth the following spring. However, mallows are best if planted fresh each spring. They can be grown from cuttings taken in fall and stored in a protected spot in the garden, such as under the eaves of the house. Start new plants from those cuttings in spring.

'Silver Cup' (above), 'Mont Blanc' (below)

L. maritima (L. bicolor) is a shrub that grows 4–8' tall and spreads 3–4' wide. It has maple-like gray foliage. The light pink flowers have dark centers and dark pink veins and bloom profusely all spring, summer and fall. This plant needs regular light pruning during the season to keep it at its best. It will tolerate full sun in all but the hot Central Valley climates.

L. thuringiaca **'Barnsley'** is a perennial that grows 6' tall and wide and bears red-centered white flowers from spring to fall.

Problems & Pests

Plant in well-drained soil to avoid root rot. Destroy any rust-infected plants.

All mallows are a good choice for seaside gardens because they tolerate coastal conditions.

'Silver Cup' (above)

Marigold
Tagetes

Height: 7"–4' **Spread:** 12–24" **Flower color**: yellow, red, gold, orange, cream and bicolors

MARIGOLDS are considered sacred by Hindus in India and other parts of the world. My father saved seed every year from a dwarf variety of *Tagetes patula*. I discovered a jar of these seeds when I was cleaning up my dad's home after his death. I scattered the seeds over the graves of both my mother and father in Loomis. The cemetery groundskeepers, who practice the Hindu religion, make sure the marigolds on my parents' gravesite bloom every year. That is sacred to me.

Planting

Seeding: Direct sow in spring or indoors earlier

Transplanting: Once soil has warmed; best from six-packs

Spacing: Dwarf marigolds, 6"; tall marigolds, 12"

Growing

Marigolds grow best in **full sun.** The soil should be of **average fertility** and **well drained.** These plants are drought tolerant.

Deadhead to encourage more flowers and to keep the plants tidy.

Tips

Mass planted or mixed with other plants, marigolds make a vibrant addition to beds, borders and container gardens. These plants will thrive in the hottest, driest parts of your garden.

T. tenuifolia (this page)

T. tenuifolia *is used as a culinary or tea herb in some Latin American countries.*

T. patula

Recommended

T. erecta (African Marigold; Aztec Marigold; American Marigold) grows 3–4' tall and bears huge flowers but is not often found. The cultivars are more readily available. 'Cracker Jack' series bears large, double flowers in bright shades of orange and yellow on tall plants that grow to 36". 'Inca' plants are compact, up to 18" tall, and bear double flowers in solid or multi-colored shades of yellow, gold and orange. 'Marvel' is a compact cultivar, growing only 18" tall, but with the large flowers that make this species popular. 'Vanilla' bears cream-white flowers on compact, odorless plants.

T. patula (French Marigold) is low-growing, only 7–10" tall. 'Bonanza' series is another popular double-flowered cultivar. Its flowers are red, orange, yellow and bicolored. 'Janie' series is a popular double-flowered cultivar. It is an early-blooming, compact plant with red, orange and yellow blooms.

T. tenuifolia (Signet Marigold) has dainty, single flowers that grow on bushy plants with feathery foliage. 'Gem' series is commonly available. The compact plants, about 10" tall, bear flowers continuously all summer in shades of yellow and orange.

T. erecta and T. patula are often used in vegetable gardens for their reputed insect-repelling abilities.

T. **Triploid Hybrids** (Triploid Marigolds) have been developed by crossing African Marigold and French Marigold. The resulting plants have the huge flowers of African Marigold and the compact growth of French Marigold. These hybrids are the most heat resistant of all the marigolds. They generally grow about 12" tall and spread 12–24". 'Nugget' bears large yellow, red, orange, gold or bicolored flowers on low, wide-spreading plants.

Problems & Pests

Slugs and snails can eat seedlings to the ground. Established plants may experience attacks of whiteflies or spider mites when stressed. Maintain regular watering and use an oil spray to eliminate this problem.

T. erecta (above), *T. patula* (below)

When using marigolds as cut flowers, remove the lower leaves to take away some of the pungent scent.

Mexican Sunflower

Tithonia

Height: 4–6' **Spread:** 2–4' **Flower color:** orange, red-orange, yellow-orange

FOR THAT 'HOT' LOOK IN THE GARDEN, Mexican Sunflower is one of the best plants you can grow. It does well in sunny coastal climates as well as the HOT, HOT interior valleys. It makes a great combination with tall marigolds, Sunflower, cosmos and Butterfly Weed. Mixing it in a border with *Salvia* 'Red Hot Sally' gives a great blast of color that attracts butterflies and hummingbirds.

Planting

Seeding: Direct sow mid-March through April; indoors earlier

Transplanting: Mid-March to July

Spacing: 24"

Growing

Mexican Sunflower grows best in **full sun.** The soil should be of **average to poor fertility, moist** and **well drained.** Cover seeds lightly because they germinate more evenly and quickly when exposed to some light. Mexican Sunflower needs little water or care; however, it will bloom more profusely if it is deadheaded regularly.

Sear ends of cut flowers with a flame.

Tips

Mexican Sunflower is heat resistant, so it is ideal for growing in a sunny, warm spot in your garden. The plants are tall and break easily if exposed to too much wind; grow along a wall or fence to provide shelter and stability. These annuals are coarse in appearance and are well suited to the back of a border where they can provide a good backdrop to a bed of shorter annuals.

Recommended

T. rotundifolia is a vigorous, bushy plant. It grows 4–6' tall and spreads 2–4'. Vibrant orange-red flowers are produced from mid- to late summer through to frost. '**Goldfinger**' grows to 48" tall and bears large orange flowers. '**Torch**' has bright red-orange flowers. '**Yellow Torch**' has bright yellow flowers.

Problems & Pests

This plant is generally resistant to most problems; however, young foliage may suffer slug and snail damage. Aphids can become a real problem, usually in early spring. If the aphids are washed off a couple of times, the problem ceases as warm weather takes over. Whiteflies may also cause problems.

Million Bells
Calibrachoa

Height: 6–12" **Spread**: up to 24" **Flower color:** pink, purple, yellow, orange, red, blue, white

MILLION BELLS AND PETUNIAS were discovered at the same time, and it is thought that they were discovered in Brazil. Petunias made an instant hit and were hybridized for larger blooms and all sorts of growth habits. Million Bells, however, didn't come into its own until it was 'rediscovered' by Euro-American propagators. It is now the most popular annual for many floral applications, especially hanging baskets.

Planting

Seeding: Seeds may not be available

Transplanting: After last frost

Spacing: 6–15"

Growing

Million Bells prefers to grow in **full sun to light shade**. The soil should be **fertile, moist** and **well drained**. Though it prefers to be watered regularly, Million Bells is fairly drought resistant in cool and warm climates. Pinch back the tips to keep plants compact. Million Bells will bloom well into fall; it develops hardiness as the weather cools and can survive temperatures down to 20° F.

Tips

Popular for planters and hanging baskets, Million Bells is also attractive in beds and borders where its trailing habit will allow it to blend between other plants. This plant grows all summer and needs plenty of room to spread or it will overtake other flowers. In a hanging basket, it will toll out multitudes of bell-shaped blooms.

Recommended

Calibrachoa hybrids are a new and distinct species developed from petunias and other plants. Plants in the 'Colorburst' series are compact and mounding and bloom in shades of red, rose and purple. 'Million Bells' series includes 'Trailing Blue' with dark blue or purple flowers with yellow centers, 'Trailing Pink' with rose pink, yellow centered flowers and 'Trailing White' with white, yellow centered flowers. 'Terracotta' has reddish orange flowers, and 'Yellow' has bright yellow flowers; these two unique colors truly distinguish Million Bells from petunias.

Problems & Pests

Wet weather and cloudy days could cause leaf spot and delayed blooming. Watch for slugs and earwigs. Budworm is a major problem. Use B.t. or pick the worms off in early morning.

Moss Rose
Portulaca

Height: 4–8" **Spread:** 12–18" **Flower color:** red, pink, yellow, white, orange

MOSS ROSE is a wonderfully satisfying low-growing annual. It looks great in rock gardens, window boxes and moss baskets. Moss Rose combined with dwarf zinnias and dwarf marigolds brings a lot of hot colors to a full-sun garden. All of these plants are relatively free from insects.

A direct relative of Moss Rose is Purslane, another plant in the *Portulaca* genus. It's infamous for its ability to multiply. The French use Purslane in soup, and Italians eat it in fresh salads. One of my employees discovered some growing as weeds at the nursery and took bag after bag of it home to his Italian grandmother. After about six weeks it completely disappeared. He wanted to plant seeds, but I told him politely, 'Don't bother.'

Planting

Seeding: Indoors in late winter

Transplanting: Once soil has warmed; use six-packs for quick results

Spacing: 12"

Growing

Moss Rose requires **full sun**. The soil should be of **poor fertility, sandy, well drained** and somewhat dry. The bed should have sufficient **organic matter** to allow water to penetrate. Avoid high nitrogen fertilizers. Weekly watering is sufficient for the interior valleys. In other areas, if the flowers wilt, a sprinkle of water will revive them quickly. When it comes to watering Moss Rose, less is better.

If you seed outdoors after the last frost date, the tiny seeds may get washed away in rainstorms, and plants will pop up in unexpected places. Use a seed cover to keep seed in place. Moss Rose is easy to start from cuttings.

Spacing the plants close together is not a problem; in fact, it causes them to intermingle, resulting in well-mixed flower colors.

Tips

Moss Rose is the ideal plant for garden spots that just don't get enough water. It is great for people who like having baskets hanging from the front porch but always forget to water. As long as the location is sunny, the plants will do well with minimal care.

Moss Rose has a habit of looking shabby after its initial bloom. Try scattering seed over blooming plants to allow new plants to take over.

Recommended

P. grandiflora forms a bushy mound of succulent foliage. It bears

delicate, papery, rose-like flowers profusely all summer. **'Cloudbeater'** bears large double flowers in many colors. The flowers stay open all day. **'Magic Carpet'** series produces double flowers in red, orange, yellow, pink and white. Sometimes the flowers are striped. **'Sundial'** series has long-lasting double flowers.

Problems & Pests

Snails may be a problem; preventative measures are advised.

Nasturtium
Indian Cress
Tropaeolum

Height: 10–24" for dwarf varieties; 8–15' for trailing varieties
Spread: equal to or wider than height **Flower color:** red, orange, yellow, pink, white, bicolored

I HAVE NOTICED THAT IF YOU PLANT NASTURTIUMS near cucumbers you will not have bitter cucumbers. I think this is because nasturtiums attract a large honeybee population. The honeybees must have known what I discovered as a child—that the spur of the flower contains a small amount of sugary-tasting nectar. I'm afraid the neighbors always wondered why their plants had no flowers!

Planting

Seeding: Direct sow during rainy season, up to mid-April; soak seeds overnight to improve germination

Transplanting: Mid-February through April; after danger of frost has passed

Spacing: 12"

Growing

Nasturtiums grow in **full sun** to **partial shade**. They do not like a lot of heat. The soil should be of **average to poor fertility, light, moist** and **well drained**. Let the soil drain completely between waterings. In the hot interior valleys, keep the plants out of the hot sun and do not let the soil dry out. On the coast, these plants can be grown all year.

Nasturtiums do best when the seeds are sown directly in the garden. Do not let the soil dry out as the seeds are germinating. Place a row cover over the bed or use mulch to help retain soil moisture. Nasturtiums will re-seed where their needs are met.

Tips

Nasturtiums are used in beds, borders, containers, hanging baskets and on sloped banks. The climbing varieties are also used to grow up trellises or over rocks on walls and other places that need concealing. These plants thrive in poor locations, and they make an interesting

Recipe: *Poor man's capers (pickled nasturtium seedpods)*

Soak green seeds in a brine made from 2 cups water and 1 tsp. salt for 24 hours.

Fill small sterilized jars with the seeds, a peeled clove of garlic and 1 tsp. pickling spices.

Heat white wine vinegar to simmering and fill each jar with the vinegar.

Seal with acid-proof lids and let the seeds sit for about a month. The pickled seeds should be eaten within a week after opening.

'Alaska' (above), 'Peach Melba' (below)

addition to plantings on hard-to-mow slopes.

Their best show is late spring to early summer or in late fall in most of Northern California. The flowers and leaves are edible and add a beautiful touch to salads. Nasturtiums are ideal under tall trees where they get morning and late afternoon sun but are out of the hot mid-day sun.

Some gardeners believe that nasturtiums attract and harbor certain pests, such as whiteflies and aphids, and that they should not be grown near plants that are susceptible to the same problems. Other gardeners believe that nasturtiums are preferred by pest insects and that the pests will flock to them and leave the rest of the garden alone. Still other gardeners claim that these plants, because of the high sulfur levels in the leaves, repel many pests that would otherwise infest the garden. I have yet to notice nasturtiums' influence, for better or worse, on the pest populations in my garden.

Recommended

T. majus has either a trailing or mounding habit. Trailing selections reach 6–10' in length. Mounding selections grow 10–18" tall and wide. Plants of this species have been greatly improved by hybridizing. The foliage of the older varieties tended to hide the flowers, but new varieties hold their flowers (available in a great selection of colors) above the foliage. There are also some new and interesting cultivars with variegated foliage and compact, attractive, mound-forming habits. **'Alaska'** series has white-marbled foliage. **'Empress of India'** is an outstanding selection growing 2' tall and bearing a profusion of bright red flowers. **'Jewel'** series has compact plants that grow to 12" tall and wide, with double flowers in a mix of deep orange, red or gold. **'Peach Melba'** forms a 12" mound. The flowers are pale yellow with a bright orange-red splash at the base of each petal. **'Whirlybird'** is a compact, bushy plant. The single or double flowers in shades of red, pink, yellow or orange do not have spurs.

T. peregrinum (Canary Vine, Canary Bird Flower) climbs 8–15' and produces bright yellow flowers from summer to fall. The common name comes from the shape of the upper flower petals, which are larger than the lower petals and fringed, resembling the wings of a tiny bird. This species prefers light shade.

Problems & Pests

Aphids, slugs, whiteflies and some viruses can afflict nasturtiums. Washing off foliage routinely will alleviate most problems. Nasturtiums are deer resistant in most landscapes.

Nasturtiums have a place in the vegetable or herb garden. The leaves and flowers are edible and can be added to salads, soups and dips to add a peppery flavor. The unripe seeds can be pickled and used as a substitute for capers (see recipe p. 189).

'Alaska' (above), *T. majus* (below)

Nemesia
Nemesia

Height: 8–12" **Spread:** 4–10" **Flower color:** white, yellow, pink, orange, red, blue, purple

I FIND NEMESIA to be one of the finest bulb bed covers. It thrives in cool weather in the interior valleys but will burn away if the temperature remains consistently above 80° F. An occasional blast of heat will set the plant back temporarily, but it will recover. Along the coast it can be used all year in hanging baskets, containers and as an accent around established plantings.
The bright colors enrich the garden.

Planting

Seeding: Direct sowing not recommended; start indoors in mid-winter or early spring

Transplanting: April to May in warm soil; from six-packs or 4" pots; available in fall in one-gallon containers

Spacing: 6"

Growing

Nemesia prefers **full sun**. The soil should be **fertile, moist, neutral to acidic** and **well drained**. The plants need regular water during hot, dry weather.

Deadhead Nemesia to prolong its blooming. Pinch tips when plant is young to promote a bushy form.

Nemesia may be slow to start and may fade a bit during the hottest part of summer, so group it with plants that will fill in the space. As the weather cools in late summer, Nemesia will revive and start flowering.

Tips

This bushy plant makes an attractive addition to rock gardens, mixed containers, baskets and annual beds.

Recommended

N. strumosa is a compact, bushy plant that blooms in mid- to late summer. Flowers may be single or bicolored in shades of purple, pink, blue, yellow, white or red. '**Carnival**' is a compact plant with yellow, red, pink, orange or white flowers with purple veins. '**KLM**' has bicolored flowers that are blue and white with yellow centers.

Problems & Pests

To avoid root rot, water plants in the morning only and let them dry out during foggy days. If wilted, Nemesia will recover rapidly.

Ornamental Kale
Brassica

Height: 12–24" **Spread:** 12–24" **Flower color:** grown for foliage

THE MOST BEAUTIFUL ORNAMENTAL KALE I have seen was grown in Alaska, with the heads of the plant averaging 2' across. There they grow this plant during summer. Here in Northern California I like to toss the seed of this winter annual into an area and just let it grow. I thin and transplant the plants when they have six to seven true leaves. I wash the soil off the root using a transplanting liquid and plant them as bare-root plants. In the Bay Area do the transplanting on a foggy day, not on a hot day. Most of the plants will recover in a day or two and grow wonderfully.

Planting

Seeding: Direct sow from September to October

Transplanting: September; from six-packs

Spacing: 18–24"

Growing

Ornamental Kale prefers to grow in **full sun** but tolerates partial shade. The soil should be **fertile, well drained** and **moist**. Ornamental Kale also prefers soil with a **neutral to slightly alkaline pH,** which is what we have in most of Northern California. For best results, side dress with organic fertilizer from September through March.

Ornamental Kale can be started in seedbeds or trays and transplanted in fall. Many packages of seeds contain a variety of cultivars.

The plant colors brighten after a light frost or when the air temperature drops below 50° F.

'Sunset' (above), 'Snow Prince' (below)

Nothing says 'I love you' like a dozen long-stemmed cabbages! 'Sunrise' and 'Sunset' are grown for their long-stemmed, rose-like appearance.

Ornamental Kale is related to cabbage and broccoli and makes a colorful addition to any salad. The oldest leaves may be somewhat bitter.

Tips

Ornamental Kale is a tough, bold plant that is at home in the vegetable garden as well as in the border of flowerbeds.

Wait until some true leaves develop before thinning. When thinning seedlings, those that are not transplanted can be used in salad.

Recommended

B. oleracea (Acephala Group) forms loose, erect rosettes of large, often fringed leaves in shades of purple, red, pink and white. It grows 12–24" tall with an equal spread. Plants of this species are biennials, producing flowers in shades of white to yellow in the second year. '**Color-up**' mix is very fast to color up and slow to send up its spike. The plants grow 10" tall and 12" wide. Inner leaves come in colors of red, pink and white. '**Nagoya**' has frilled foliage and colorful inner foliage over an extended period. The inner foliage comes in red, white and rose. The plants grow 12" tall and spread 12–18". '**Osaka**' grows 12" tall and wide with wavy foliage, red to pink in the center and blue-green to the outside. '**Peacock**' grows 15–18" tall and 18" wide. The leaves are finely frilled. The inner leaves may be red or white, and the outer leaves are green. '**Red on Green**' has fringed foliage. The inner leaves are light to dark pink and the outer leaves are green. The leaf veins are cream on the outer leaves fading to pink on the inner leaves. '**Snow Prince**' has

'White Peacock'

variegated green and cream leaves and salmon pink centers. '**Sunrise**' and '**Sunset**' are new small-headed, long-stemmed plants used as long-lasting cut flowers. They grow up to 24" tall. The central leaves of 'Sunrise' are creamy white with a pink tinge in the very center. 'Sunset' has red-colored foliage.

Problems & Pests

Ornamental Kale is affected by a large range of pests and diseases including caterpillars, leaf miners, aphids, root maggots, cabbage worm (white butterfly), nematodes, plant bugs, flea beetles, leaf spot, clubroot and damping off. Ornamental Kale may also suffer nutrient deficiency problems.

Mixed planting (below)

Painted Daisy
Chrysanthemum
Chrysanthemum

Height: 8–36" **Spread:** 8–36" **Flower color:** white, red, yellow, pink or purple, multi-colored

PAINTED DAISIES ARE GREAT FOR BORDERS or cut-flower beds. They combine well with zinnias, salvias and other heat-loving plants. As cut flowers, painted daisies can stand alone or add vivid color to any bouquet. I have used *C. coccineum* as a flea repellent around my doghouses. It seemed to work because when I changed the dogs' bedding there were never any fleas.

Planting

Seeding: Direct sow or sow seed indoors in spring

Transplanting: Late February to mid-April

Spacing: *C. carinatum* and *C. coccineum* 10"; *C. paludosum* 6–8"

Growing

Painted daisies prefer **full sun** but tolerate partial shade. The soil should be of **average fertility** and **well drained**. A second sowing in mid-summer will bring late-season flowers. Deadhead to prolong the blooming period.

Tips

Painted daisies are brightly colored additions to the informal bed or border. They are sturdy plants and can help support tall plants that often require staking.

'Court Jesters' (opposite page),
C. carinatum (this page)

Recommended

C. carinatum (Tricolor Chrysanthemum, Painted Daisy) is an upright plant that grows 24–36" tall, 24–36" wide and blooms from late summer to fall. The most common flower colors are red, yellow, white or purple; the centers, petal bases and petal tips are often banded in different colors. It has become naturalized and is somewhat weedy along Southern California's coast. '**Court Jesters**' has many colors, with the petal bases banded in orange or red. '**Rainbow**' series has many colors, with two bands at the petal bases.

C. coccineum (Leucanthemum coccineum, Pyrethrum coccineum, Pyrethrum roseum) (Pyrethrum, Painted Daisy) grows 18–36" tall and 18" wide. Single, large, yellow-centered flowers in red, pink or white bloom in spring. Planting this species around doghouses and other outdoor animal shelters will keep fleas away from bedding areas.

C. paludosum (Leucanthemum paludosum, Melampodium paludosum) is a compact plant growing 8–10" tall and 8" wide. It bears yellow to white flowers with deep yellow centers in summer.

Problems & Pests

Aphids love these flowers and should be washed off with insecticidal soap or a brisk spray from the garden hose.

Painted daisies make long-lasting and popular cut flowers. In Victorian flower symbolism, a white painted daisy represented truth and a yellow one indicated slighted love.

Painted-Tongue
Velvet Flower
Salpiglossis

Height: 24–36" **Spread:** 12" **Flower color:** shades of red, yellow, orange, pink, blue, purple, brown; often patterned bicolors

PAINTED-TONGUE is remarkable for its deeply veined flowers and many unusual colors and color combinations. Use Painted-tongue where the afternoon sun will backlight the vibrant colors of the flowers. Place plants close together so they can help support each other. The plants do well in baskets and combine well with Bacopa, sweet potato vine and verbena plants.

The iridescent quality of these flowers causes their color to change as they turn in a breeze.

Planting

Seeding: Direct sowing not recommended; seed indoors in late winter in peat pots or pellets

Transplanting: Late March; from six-packs

Spacing: 12"

Growing

Painted-tongue prefers **full sun.** The soil should be **fertile,** rich in **organic matter, moist** and **well drained.** The seeds are very tiny and shouldn't be covered with soil. They will germinate more evenly if kept in darkness until they sprout—cover pots with dark plastic or layers of newspaper or place pots in a dark closet. Keep seeds warm. Once they start to sprout, the plants can be moved into light. If direct sowing, use a row cover. Leave the cover on until the seedlings begin to push against it. In cool weather remove the cover during the day and replace it at night. Remove the cover completely when seedlings reach 2" tall.

Tips

Painted-tongue is useful in the middle or back of beds and borders. It can also be used in large mixed containers. Painted-tongue can become battered in rainy and windy conditions. Plant it in warm, sheltered areas of the garden.

Recommended

S. sinuata is an upright plant related to petunias. **'Blue Peacock'** has blue flowers with yellow throats and dark veins. **'Casino'** series has flowers in a wide range of colors. It blooms early

and tolerates rain and wind. **'Royal Mix'** is somewhat more compact, growing 12–16" tall. The flowers come in a range of solids and bi-colors including red, dark red, blue, pale blue, orange, purple, chocolate brown and yellow.

Problems & Pests

Aphids or root rot are possible problems. Allow the soil to dry out between waterings.

Petunia
Petunia

Height: 6–24" **Spread:** 12–36" **Flower color:** pink, purple, red, white, yellow or bicolored in singles and doubles

PETUNIAS have lost some of their popularity over the years because of budworm, but there are ways of defending against this critter. The adult moth lays its eggs at night while in flight. It literally dusts plants, including petunias, geraniums, flowering tobacco and others, with eggs. As the eggs hatch, the larvae attack and enter the flower buds, where they cannot be reached by any insecticide. Other than handpicking the worms in the morning, try covering your petunias with cheesecloth, a row cover or a seed blanket at night and removing the cover in the morning. The hatching eggs will not get to the plants. Despite the budworm and necessary protective measures, petunias are wonderful plants that add vibrant color to the garden.

Planting

Seeding: Indoors in mid-winter

Transplanting: After last frost

Spacing: 12–18"

Growing

Petunias prefer **full sun**. The soil should be of **poor to average fertility, sandy** and **well drained**. When sowing, press seeds into soil surface but don't cover them with soil. Pinch halfway back in mid-summer to keep plants bushy and encourage new growth and flowers.

Use lots of compost to increase drainage in heavy clay soils. Commercial planting mix can also be used if compost is not available.

'Ultra' grandiflora (above), milliflora (below)

Aphids and fungus may also be problems. The fungal problems can be avoided by not wetting the foliage, if possible, and by providing a location with good drainage.

Tips

Use petunias in beds, borders, containers and hanging baskets. Even the most neglected petunia plants will continue to bloom all summer.

If you would like to grow a multitude of different varieties, it is best to transplant from six-packs.

Recommended

P. x *hybrida* is a large group of popular annuals that fall into three categories: the grandifloras, the multifloras and the millifloras.

The **grandiflora** petunias have the largest flowers—up to 4" across. They have the widest variety of colors and forms, but they are the most likely to be damaged by heavy rain. They grow 12–24" tall and 24–36" wide. **'Daddy'** series is available in darkly veined shades of pink and purple. **'Supercascade'** series is

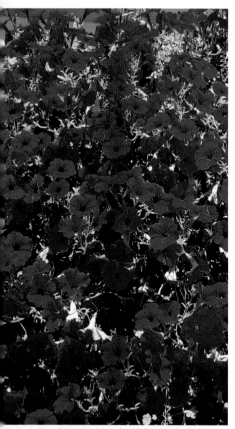

'Purple Wave' (above), milliflora (below)

available in a wide variety of colors. Plants in this series work best in large planters where the cascading effect is spectacular. '**Ultra**' series is available in many colors, including bicolors. This cultivar recovers quite quickly from weather damage.

The **multiflora** petunias have smaller flowers, about half the size of the grandifloras, bear many more flowers and are more tolerant of adverse weather conditions. The plants are around the same size as the grandifloras. '**Carpet**' series is available in a wide variety of colors. '**Wave**' series is available in pink and purple. This plant is popular for hanging baskets and containers. It recovers well from rain damage, blooms a lot and spreads quickly.

The **milliflora** petunias are the newest group. The flowers, about 1" across, are borne profusely over the whole plant. These petunias tolerate wet weather very well and some-times self-seed. '**Fantasy**' series is available in shades of red, purple, pink and white, although the pinks tend to be the easiest to find. With this type's growing popularity, more colors will likely become available. These petunias are popular in mixed containers and hanging baskets and are very nice in garden beds, form-ing neat mounds of foliage and flowers. These self-grooming plants are one of the best bets for neat mass plantings, giving the impression of Busy Lizzie Impatiens in the sun.

The following cultivars are 2002 All American Selections winners. They tolerate severe weather and do not require pinching and pruning.

'**Lavender Wave**' grows 4–6" tall and spreads up to 4' wide. It produces profuse lavender flowers all summer and is quite heat tolerant. '**Tidal Wave Silver**' is a hedgiflora type petunia; the height it grows to depends on how far the plants are spaced apart. With support such as a trellis they can grow 3' tall. If spaced at 12" they grow 16–22" tall and 18" wide. If spaced at 24" they grow 12" tall and spread 3' wide. The plants bear silvery white to pale lavender flowers with darker purple throats and slightly darker petal veins. They are gray mold tolerant.

Problems & Pests

Budworm it the biggest problem for petunias. You can use B.t. but it may blast the buds. Handpick the worms off the plants **daily**.

'Tidal Wave Silver' (above),
multiflora 'Lavender Wave' (below)

Phlox
Phlox

Height: 6–18" **Spread:** 10" or more **Flower color:** purple, pink, red, blue, white, yellow

THE EXTRA BRIGHT COLORS OF PHLOX make it a popular addition to any annual flowerbed. In most areas on the coastal plain it is good for year-round color. In the cooler coastal climates, Phlox is best planted in June through August and then again in February for spring color. In the hot interior valleys Phlox does best from late winter through early spring and will be under stress when the temperatures soar from June through August. In these areas it is best to use this plant as a winter annual, planting seed in September or transplanting from six-packs in October.

Planting

Seeding: On the coast, direct sow mid-March through mid-June, indoors earlier; in the interior, direct sow in September

Transplanting: On the coast, June through August and again in February; in the interior, October; from six-packs

Spacing: Up to 8"

Growing

Phlox prefers **full sun**. The soil should be **fertile, humus rich, moist** and **well drained**. Check the roots of transplants to make sure that they aren't root-bound; if they are, score the rootball on two sides with a sharp knife. Plant cuttings in moist soil and they will easily root. Phlox plants can be spaced quite close together. Deadhead to promote blooming.

Tips

Use Phlox in beds, borders, containers, rock gardens and on rock walls. To discourage disease, do not overwater.

Recommended

P. drummondii forms a bushy plant that can be upright or spreading and bears clusters of white, purple, pink or red flowers from early summer to frost. '**Coral Reef**' bears attractive pastel-colored flowers. '**Paloma**' series is compact, growing 8–10" tall. This plant blooms heavily, and the flowers come in many colors, often with contrasting centers. '**Twinkle**' mixed has unusual small, star-shaped flowers on compact plants 8" tall. The colors of the petal margins and the centers often contrast with the main petal color.

Problems & Pests

To avoid fungal problems, provide good drainage and don't let water stand on the leaves late in the day. Check for spider mites in mid-summer.

Pincushion Flower

Scabiosa

Height: 12–36" **Spread:** 9–12" or more **Flower color:** purple, red, maroon, blue, pink, white

I ONCE HAD A PINCUSHION FLOWER plant in a 4" pot and forgot about it because it was not in a location I walked by every day. The poor plant was almost dead when I finally watered it and moved it to a location in full sun. The little plant forgave me and produced an abundance of wonderful blue flowers for the rest of the summer. Pincushion flowers are excellent for a cut-flower bed and look great mixed with blue Lobelia, Sweet Alyssum, dwarf white Spider Flower or mixed zinnias.

Planting

Seeding: Indoors in late winter; direct sow in mid-spring

Transplanting: Mid-March through May

Spacing: 9–12"

Growing

Pincushion flower plants grow best in **full sun**. The soil should be of **average to rich fertility,** have plenty of **organic matter** and be **well drained**.

Tips

Pincushion flowers are useful in beds, borders and mixed containers. The flowers are also popular for use in fresh arrangements. The plants do not need a lot of water to produce an abundance of flowers.

Recommended

S. atropurpurea is an upright, branching plant that grows 30–36" tall and 12" wide. The tall stems may fall over as the plants mature. Insert twiggy branches into the ground around the plants when they are small to give them support as they grow taller. The flowers of this species may be white, blue, red or purple. '**Imperial Giants**' bears blooms in a deep maroon color as well as shades of pink.

S. stellata grows 18" tall and spreads half as much. This plant bears small, white flowers but is grown for its papery, orb-like seedpods which dry in unusual globe shapes and are useful accents in dried arrangements. Pick *S. stellata* while still slightly green to keep dried seedpods from shattering. '**Paper Moon**' ('**Drumstick**') bears blue flowers that dry to a warm bronze color.

The densely petaled blooms serve as a perfect landing pad for butterflies.

Poor Man's Orchid
Butterfly Flower
Schizanthus

Height: 6–18" **Spread:** 9–12" **Flower color:** pink, red, orange, yellow, white or purple; yellow throats marked with streaks and blotches

AS A CALIFORNIAN, I always get a kick out of flower books that say a certain plant should be grown in fertile, well-drained soil. I don't know where there is any fertile, well-drained soil in the entire state of California, much less the northern part! Poor Man's Orchid, however, needs fertile, well-drained soil, so for every cubic foot of soil add two cubic feet of organic matter. The organic matter will lead to an increase in soil bioactivity, a healthier root zone and healthier plants.

Planting

Seeding: Indoors 4–6 weeks before last frost; direct sow around last frost date

Transplanting: March through June for extended flowering period

Spacing: 12"

Growing

Poor Man's Orchid grows best in **light or dappled shade**. The soil should be **fertile, moist** and **well drained**. This plant does not tolerate frost or excess heat but does quite well planted in light shade.

The seeds should be planted on the soil surface. Keep the entire container in darkness or cover it with dark plastic or newspaper to promote even germination. When sowing directly, use a row cover to give the plants a head start. Remove the cover once the seeds have sprouted.

These plants have a short flowering season, but you can extend the bloom time with successive sowings. Alternatively, you can replace them halfway through summer with chrysanthemums that bloom in late summer and fall.

The flowers of Poor Man's Orchid are colorful and long lasting after they are cut, making them a good choice for fresh arrangements.

Tips

Poor Man's Orchid can be used in beds, borders, rock gardens, hanging baskets and mixed containers. It does best in cool summer climates. It is an ideal plant for coastal regions and an early bloomer in the hotter valley areas. This plant combines well with Creeping Zinnia and most other annuals.

Poor Man's Orchid can be grown as a temporary indoor potted plant in a bright, sunny window. Don't over-water plants indoors, and never put a tray containing water underneath the plant.

The alternate common name, Butterfly Flower, is a reference to the blooms' resemblance to butterflies, not their ability to attract them.

Recommended

S. pinnatus is an erect plant with light green, fern-like leaves. The brightly colored flowers bloom for an extended period from spring to fall. '**Dwarf Bouquet**' mixed are shorter, more compact plants, growing to 16", and are good container plants. The flowers are shades of red, orange, pink and orange-yellow. '**Royal Pierrot**' mixed plants have rich colors in pink, purple, purple-blue and white and are good in hanging baskets. '**Star Parade**' is a compact variety available in several colors. It grows up to 10" tall.

Poppy
Papaver

Height: 10–36" **Spread**: 6–12" **Flower color:** red, pink, white, purple, yellow, orange

MY WIFE AND I VISITED THE NETHERLANDS in April 2000. It wasn't the right time to see the red poppies that Canadian John McCrae wrote about in his wonderful poem 'In Flanders Fields,' eulogizing the soldiers who died and were buried there during WWI. Still, I could imagine the poppies blowing the way McCrae had described them. At one time American veterans sold tissue paper poppies at stores, both to remind us that these people fought for our freedom and to raise money for the many veteran organizations throughout the country. These lovely flowers, also called Shirley Poppies, re-seed themselves freely and are an outstanding addition to any cottage garden.

Planting

Seeding: Direct sow in fall and every two weeks in spring

Spacing: 6–12"

Growing

Poppies grow best in **full sun.** The soil should be **fertile, sandy** and have lots of **organic matter** mixed in. The pH should be 6.5 to 7.5. If your soil is too acidic, add oyster shell lime or dolomite lime.

Good drainage is essential. Starting seeds indoors is not recommended because transplanting is often unsuccessful. Mix the tiny seeds with fine sand for even sowing. Deadhead to prolong blooms.

Tips

Poppies are useful in mixed borders where other plants are slow to fill in. Poppies will fill in empty spaces early in the season; then the foliage dies back over summer, leaving

P. rhoeas (above), *P. croceum* (below)

The seeds of Shirley Poppy can be used to flavor baked goods such as muffins, breads and bagels.

P. croceum (above)

P. rhoeas (center & below)

room for other plants. They can also be used in rock gardens, and the cut flowers are popular for fresh arrangements.

Be careful when weeding around faded summer plants; you may accidentally pull up late summer poppy seedlings. *P. croceum* and *P. rhoeas* will self-seed.

Sow seeds of *P. croceum* in late August through September for late-fall to early-spring flowers. The flowers tolerate cold temperatures to 25° F and also will recover from heavy storms. *P. croceum* is best used as an annual for winter color because the plants tend to rot out in summer. This species is great as a picking flower.

Recommended

P. commutatum (Greek Poppy) grows 18" tall and spreads 6–12". Abundant bright red, cup-shaped blooms appear for a few weeks in mid-summer. Each petal has a black spot near its base.

P. croceum (*P. nudicaule*) (Iceland Poppy) is a short-lived perennial from northern climates that is grown as an annual. The plants reach a height of 12–24" and spread about 6". The large, cup-shaped flowers come in shades of yellow, orange, rose, pink, cream and white. 'Champagne Bubbles' is a strong, bushy plant, with lots of pastel flowers. 'Wonderland' is a hardy selection that grows to 10" tall and produces flowers in shades of red, orange, yellow and white. The flowers smell like fresh pumpkin.

P. rhoeas (Shirley Poppy, Flanders Field Poppy) forms a basal rosette of foliage about 12" wide. Its flowers, held well above the foliage, are borne on stems 24–36" long. 'Mother of Pearl' bears flowers in pastel pinks and purples. 'Shirley' series flowers have silky, cup-shaped petals. The flowers come in many colors and can be single, double or semi-double.

Problems & Pests

Poppies rarely have problems, although fungal problems can occur if the soil is wet and poorly drained.

P. rhoeas (above), *P. croceum* (below)

For cut flowers, stick the cut end of each stem in a flame or boiling water to seal it.

Pot Marigold
Calendula, English Marigold
Calendula

Height: 10–24" **Spread:** 8–20" **Flower color:** yellow, orange, cream, apricot, gold

CALENDULA was originally grown primarily as a bitter herb and secondarily for its color. It is one of the brightest colored flowers that one could have for the winter garden, with the color usually lasting well into spring. The name Pot Marigold refers to its use in Switzerland where it was used in pots so that it could be moved into a protected spot in case of heavy weather.

Pot Marigold flowers can be cut for arrangements. They combine well with Iceland Poppies.

Planting

Seeding: Direct sow in late August through September for winter blooms, in February for spring blooms

Transplanting: February for early-spring to early-summer flowers, fall for winter flowers; from six-packs or 4" pots

Spacing: 8–10"

Growing

Pot Marigold does equally well in **full sun** or **partial shade**. It likes cool weather and can withstand a light frost. The soil should be of **average fertility** and **well drained.** Pot Marigold is quick and easy to grow from seed, and many gardeners grow it that way. Young plants are readily available as transplants in the fall in most nurseries.

Deadhead to prolong blooming and keep plants looking neat.

Tips

Pot Marigold is attractive in borders, in mixed planters and in the vegetable patch. This cold-hardy annual often continues flowering until late spring, when the hot weather arrives. Pull the plants and replace them with heat-tolerant plants for the summer. The larger varieties are used as cut flowers.

Recommended

C. officinalis is a vigorous, tough, upright plant; it bears single or double daisy-like flowers in a wide range of yellow and orange shades. This plant grows 12–24" tall, with a slightly lesser spread. 'Bon Bon' is a

dwarf plant that grows 10–12" tall and comes in all colors. '**Fiesta Gitana**' ('Gypsy Festival') is a dwarf plant with flowers in a wide range of colors. '**Pacific Beauty**' is a larger plant, growing about 18" tall. It bears large flowers in varied colors.

Problems & Pests

Possible problems are aphids, whiteflies, slugs and snails, powdery mildew and fungal leaf spot.

Prickly Poppy
Argemone

Height: 3–5' **Spread:** 12–24" **Flower color:** yellow, orange

THE APTLY NAMED PRICKLY POPPY is a wonderful plant to use where you don't want a lot of traffic. This would be an ideal plant to use to stop foot traffic from crossing the corner of a lawn, but don't plant it near any window that needs to be washed periodically. If you walk through it once, you won't ever do it again. It is a practical as well as beautiful plant. The flowers hold up well as cut flowers, but wear gloves when you collect them.

Planting

Seeding: Direct sow in spring; indoors a few weeks earlier

Transplanting: Once soil has warmed

Spacing: 12–16"

Growing

Prickly Poppy prefers to grow in **full sun** in **well-drained** soil of **average to poor fertility.** Prickly Poppy likes hot locations; a location against a south- or west-facing wall, where other plants tend to wilt, suits this plant nicely.

Prickly Poppy plants don't like to have their roots disturbed. If direct sowing, plant them into their permanent locations outdoors or start them indoors in peat pots to avoid disturbing the roots when transplanting.

Prickly Poppy self-seeds and will spread over time. Deadheading will keep the plants blooming and looking good and reduce self-seeding.

Tips

Prickly Poppy is most attractive mixed into the middle and back of a border. It also makes an effective barrier plant under windows and along property lines, because the prickles can be unpleasant to walk through. Prickly Poppy makes an excellent show on hot dry banks as long as you water the plants about once a week.

Because this plant self-seeds so readily, it can form a barrier year after year.

Recommended

A. mexicana is a clump-forming plant that produces pale to deep yellow or orange flowers in late summer and early fall. The leaves have spines along the edges and at the tip.

Problems & Pests

Downy mildew and bacterial leaf spot are possible problems. Water in the morning only.

If you venture to open the very prickly seedpods, you should not eat the seeds because they can cause stomach upset.

Rock Cress
Wall Rock Cress
Arabis

Height: 6–12" **Spread:** 12–20" **Flower color:** white, pink

ROCK CRESS is sometimes considered a perennial, but it is at its best if new plants are used each year. It won't recover after a cold winter, especially as the water-holding clay soils of Northern California remain saturated during winter. Rock Cress is an exceptionally usable plant in borders, on rock walls and as a groundcover in cool coastal areas. In the interior valleys it will require some afternoon protection from the hot sun. It makes an attractive cover for spring-blooming bulbs.

Planting

Seeding: Indoors in early spring

Transplanting: Any time during growing season

Spacing: 12"

Growing

Rock Cress prefers to grow in **full sun**. The soil should be of **average or poor fertility, slightly alkaline** and **well drained**. If you are unsure of your soil's pH, get a soil test. Add horticultural lime if the soil test indicates a need. This plant will do best in a climate that doesn't have extremely hot summer weather. It is ideal for coastal planting all year long, provided the drainage is good. The seeds require light for germination.

Cut the plant back after flowering to keep it neat and compact.

Tips

Use Rock Cress in a rock garden or border or on a rock wall. It may also be used as a groundcover on an exposed slope or as a companion plant in a natural setting with small bulbs. Try Rock Cress as a winter cover crop for larger bulb beds.

Don't plant Rock Cress where it may overwhelm plants that are slower growing.

Arabis looks quite a lot like Aubrieta. *They are both commonly known as Rock Cress, so make sure you write down the botanical name of the plant you want before taking a trip to the garden center to buy it.*

Recommended

A. caucasica bears fragrant white flowers in late spring. **'Flore Pleno'** ('Plena') has double, pure white flowers. **'Pink Charm'** has pink blooms. **'Variegata'** (*A. ferdinandi-coburgi* 'Variegata') has cream-tinged or sometimes pink-tinged foliage and is a low-maintenance plant.

Problems & Pests

White rust may be a problem. If the disease is around, apply a preventative spray of horticultural oil.

Salvia
Sage
Salvia

Height: 12"–4' **Spread:** 9"–4' **Flower color:** red, blue, purple, orange, pink, white

SALVIAS ARE BECOMING MORE AND MORE POPULAR as new varieties become available. When *Salvia farinacea* 'Victoria' came on the market, I didn't know quite what to do with it—I thought it was just another sage. I found out that it grows rapidly and lends itself to any garden condition. It can tolerate wet soil for a while but appreciates drying out periodically. 'Victoria' is classified as a perennial but I have found it does not tolerate our Northern California winters. I planted it with nasturtiums, and it took the same care and added a much-needed blue texture to the planting area.

S. viridis (shown here) has been used externally to relieve sore gums. It has also been used as snuff and to flavor beers and wines.

Planting

Seeding: Indoors in mid-winter; direct sow in spring

Transplanting: Mid-March through August

Spacing: Slightly less than the plant spread

Growing

All salvia plants prefer **full sun** but some tolerate light shade. Give *S. splendens* afternoon shade in the hottest areas in the interior valleys. The soil should be **moist** and **well drained** and of **average fertility**, with lots of **organic matter**.

S. farinacea (above), *S. splendens* (below)

S. *splendens* (above), 'Victoria' (center)

S. *farinacea* (below)

Tips

Salvias look good grouped in beds and borders and in containers. The flowers are long lasting and make good cut flowers for arrangements.

To keep plants producing flowers, water often and fertilize monthly with organic compost or alfalfa tea.

Recommended

S. *coccinea* (Texas Sage) grows 24–36" tall and 24–30" wide. It bears dark pink flowers in summer. '**Coral Nymph**' has delicate, coral pink flowers on plants reaching 18–36" tall. Keep this species sheltered from the wind.

S. *farinacea* (Blue Sage; Mealy Cup Sage) grows 36–48" tall and 18–24" wide. From late spring to frost bright blue flowers are clustered along stems that look as if they are powdered with silver. This flower is also available in white. A popular cultivar of S. *farinacea* is '**Victoria**.' It is more compact than the species, growing to 18" tall and 12" wide, and has silvery foliage that makes it a beautiful addition to cut-flower arrangements. '**Victoria White**' produces white flowers.

S. *splendens* (Salvia; Scarlet Sage) is known for its spikes of bright red tubular flowers. It grows 36–48" tall with an equal spread. Recently, cultivars have become available in white, pink, purple and orange. '**Phoenix**' forms neat compact plants with flowers in bright and pastel shades of all colors. '**Red Hot Sally**' produces bright red flowers from early summer to frost. '**Salsa**' series bears solid and bicolored flowers in shades of red, orange, cream and pink. Plants in the 'Sizzler' series are compact, growing 12" tall and producing bright, early-blooming flowers in shades of red, purple, white, purple-blue and salmon pink.

S. viridis (Annual Clary Sage) is grown for its colorful bracts, not its flowers. It grows 18–24" tall and 9–12" wide and bears bracts in pink, purple, blue or white. 'Claryssa' grows to 18" tall and has brighter bracts than the species in many of the same colors.

Problems & Pests

Seedlings are prone to damping off. Aphids and a few fungal problems may occur. *S. splendens* may be attacked by Mexican giant whitefly.

Scarlet Runner Bean
Phaseolus

Height: 6–8' **Spread:** 8–10" **Flower color:** red

WHEN I FIRST PURCHASED the Belvedere Nursery, the former owner asked only one thing: to be able to harvest the beans growing at the rear of the nursery. Because there were so many pressing items to attend to, I told him it would be fine. At the time they were growing on an ugly fence with a string trellis that the plants didn't hide, and I would have pulled the plants out if I hadn't made the promise to keep them for him until the beans came. They eventually produced lovely flowers and became one of the most wonderful vines to hide an otherwise ugly fence. In addition, the beans were edible.

Planting

Seeding: Direct sow after danger of frost

Spacing: 6–8"

Growing

Scarlet Runner Bean prefers to grow in **full sun** in **well-drained, fertile, moist** soil. Ensure you provide adequate water.

Soaking the seeds in water overnight before planting helps speed up germination.

Tips

Scarlet Runner Bean is a twining climber and will need something to climb on, such as a trellis, arbor or post. Some form of lattice or netting is necessary if Scarlet Runner Bean is growing on a fence or building. Try this plant as a temporary summer screen. You can let it grow on the ground, but it is not very attractive.

Recommended

P. coccineus is a twining vine that quickly grows to a height of 6–8'. Scarlet red flowers are borne in clusters in summer. Dark green, edible pods follow flowering. 'Painted Lady' bears blooms in red and white. *P. c.* var. *alba* (Dutch Runner Bean) produces white flowers.

These plants are at home in the flower garden and the vegetable garden. The edible dark green pods are tender when young but get a little tough with age. Pick the pods just after the flowers fade for best taste in a stir-fry.

Snapdragon
Antirrhinum

Height: 14"–4' **Spread:** 8–18" **Flower color:** white, cream, yellow, orange, red, purple-red, pink or bicolored

AS A BOY, I had great luck attaching snapdragon flowers to girls' braids, much to the amusement of my male friends. I stopped the practice when a lunch bucket used my face as a target. Since then I have learned to enjoy the other wonderful merits of these plants. I like to grow snapdragons for cut flowers, especially the taller varieties such as the 'Rocket' series. Plants in the 'Rocket' series, if properly fertilized and planted in late fall, will start blooming in February and last until late spring. For colorful landscaped areas where you want varieties of colors, try the shorter strains such as 'Floral Carpet.' Snapdragons should not be planted near roses if rust is present on either plant.

Planting
Seeding: Indoors anytime; direct sow in spring

Transplanting: Anytime

Spacing: 8–18" depending on spread

Plant a row of these easy-to-please spiky flowers and introduce them to all the youngsters in your life. Squeezing the sides of the complex flowers makes them pop open like a dragon's mouth.

Growing

Snapdragons prefer **full sun** but tolerate light or partial shade. The soil should be **fertile, moist,** rich in **organic matter** and **well drained**. Snapdragons prefer a **neutral or alkaline** soil and will not perform as well in acidic soil. A raised bed allows you to easily modify the soil to accommodate the snapdragons. Sow seeds on the soil surface; do not cover them, because they require light for germination.

Tips

The height of the variety dictates the best place for the plant in the border—the shortest ones near the front and the tallest ones in the center or back of the border. The dwarf and medium-height varieties can also be used in planters, and there is even a variety available that has a droopy habit that does well in a hanging basket.

The tallest snapdragons will probably need to be staked. To encourage bushier growth, pinch the tips of the plants while they are young.

To promote further blooming and to prevent the plant from dying back before the end of the season, cut off the fading flower spikes.

Snapdragons are perennials grown as annuals. They can tolerate cold nights but rarely survive the coldest winters. Snapdragons do not enjoy the high heat in the summer months in the interior valleys but make great winter bloomers there.

Snapdragons may self-sow, providing you with new plants each year. However, the new plants may not resemble the parent plants. Planting new plants from transplants will give you the colors you want.

Recommended

Many cultivars of *A. majus* are available, with new ones introduced each year. Snapdragons are grouped into three sizes: dwarf, medium and tall. The shortest, or dwarf, varieties grow up to 12" tall and 8–12" wide. **'Floral Carpet'** is a compact, bushy dwarf selection growing 4–8" tall and 8–10" wide. It produces flowers in yellow, red, orange and pink. **'Floral Showers'** grows 6–8" tall. This compact plant bears flowers in a wide range of colors, some bicolors. **'Lampion'** is a new and interesting cultivar, usually grouped with the semi-dwarfs. It is a trailing plant that cascades up to 36". It is a great plant for hanging baskets. **'Princess'** bears white and purple bicolored flowers. This plant produces many shoots from the base and therefore many flower spikes.

Medium-height snapdragons grow 12–24" tall and up to 18" wide. **'Black Prince'** bears striking, dark, purple-red flowers set against bronze-green foliage.

The tallest cultivars, also known as giants, can grow 36–48" tall and 18" wide. **'Double Supreme'** is a tall strain bearing double, snapping flowers in a range of colors. **'Madam Butterfly'** is a tall cultivar that bears double flowers in a wide range of colors. The flowers of this cultivar don't 'snap,' as the hinged mouth structure is lost with the addition of the extra petals. **'Rocket'** series produces long spikes of brightly colored snapping flowers in many shades and is the least likely to need staking.

Problems & Pests

Snapdragons can suffer from several fungal problems including powdery mildew, fungal leaf spot, root rot, wilt and downy mildew. Snapdragon rust is the worst. To prevent rust, avoid wetting the foliage when watering, choose rust-resistant varieties and plant snapdragons in different parts of the garden each year. Aphids are sometimes a problem but can be sprayed off with water.

Spider Flower

Cleome

Height: 3–6' **Spread:** 3–5' **Flower color:** pink, rose, violet, white

I HAD A LOT OF FUN using Spider Flower in the Sonoma County Fair Garden Show one year. I put in more than 40 five-foot plants, knowing they would make a great show once they came into bloom, which was about the time they would be judged. If you look closely at the leaves, they resemble marijuana. It was so interesting see-ing the other exhibitors who were not familiar with the plant watch me put the plants in place. When the fair management questioned me, I told them what it was. When the fair was over, the plants didn't sell until I cut all the blooms off. I have used this plant on hot, dry hill-sides where it requires little or no water and on coastal parts of the northern part of the state. In the interior valleys it requires weekly watering. This wonderful plant is resistant to deer, rabbits and ground squirrels.

The flowers can be cut for fresh arrangements, although the plants have an unusual, but not unpleasant, odor that is very noticeable up close.

Planting

Seeding: Direct sow in spring for best results; indoors in late winter

Transplanting: After last frost

Spacing: 18–30"

Growing

Spider Flower prefers **full sun** but tolerates partial shade. Any kind of soil will do fine. Mix in plenty of **organic matter** to help the soil retain moisture. These plants are drought tolerant but will look and perform better if watered regularly. Don't water excessively or the plants will become leggy. Chill seeds overnight in the vegetable compartment of the refrigerator in a brown paper bag before planting.

Deadhead to prolong the blooming period and to minimize this plant's prolific self-sowing. Self-sown seedlings will start coming up almost as soon as the seeds hit the ground and can become invasive. Fortunately, the plants are distinctive and can be quickly spotted poking up where they don't belong,

'Royal Queen' (above)

Originally from South America, Spider Flower found its way to North America when President Thomas Jefferson brought the seed from France and planted it at his home in Monticello.

making them easy to pull up while they are still young.

Tips

Spider Flower can be planted in groups at the back of a border. It is also effective in the center of an island bed; use lower-growing plants around the edges to hide the leafless lower stems of Spider Flower.

Be careful when handling these plants because they have nasty barbs along the stems.

Recommended

C. hasslerana is a tall, upright plant with strong, supple stems producing clusters of flowers in summer and fall. The foliage and flowers have a strong, but not unpleasant, scent.

Spider Flower and petunias (below)

'Helen Campbell' has white flowers. 'Royal Queen' series has flowers in all colors, available by individual color or as a mixture of all available colors. The varieties are named by their color; e.g., **'Cherry Queen,'** **'Rose Queen,'** and **'Violet Queen.'** The varieties in this series are resistant to fading. **'Sparkler'** is a full, dense-growing plant reaching 3–4' in height and spreading 18–24". It bears blush pink, lavender, rose and white flowers.

Problems & Pests

Aphids may be a problem. Watch for ants, which move aphids onto plants so they can farm them for the honeydew the aphids produce.

'Helen Campbell' (above), Spider Flower and Cape Fuchsia (below)

Star Clusters
Egyptian Star
Pentas

Height: 24–36" **Spread:** 24–36" **Flower color:** pink, red, purple, white

STAR CLUSTERS IS BEST GROWN AS AN ANNUAL in the Sacramento Valley and other warm areas in Northern California. My first experience with this plant was as a houseplant. I noticed that many people were overwatering the plant, much to its dislike. For success it needs a very dry house and lots of sun. It has become naturalized in Hawaii and was originally a transplant from Africa. The blooms will last for many weeks when picked and placed in a sunny window in the house.

Planting
Seeding: Indoors in late winter or direct sow in spring

Transplanting: Late March through April

Spacing: 24"

Growing

Star Clusters grows best in **full sun** and **well-drained, moist, fertile** soil. Ensure you provide adequate water. Propagate Star Clusters plants from seed or softwood cuttings in summer. Regular deadheading will encourage more blooms.

Tips

Use Star Clusters in a bed or border where the coarse foliage provides a backdrop for smaller plants at the front of the border. Star Clusters also does very well as an outdoor container plant and is often sold during winter as a houseplant. Cuttings taken from these houseplants can be grown outside the following summer.

Pinch back the tips for a more compact, bushier plant.

Recommended

P. lanceolata is a subshrub grown as an annual. It has an erect, sometimes prostrate, growth habit and produces flat-topped clusters of pink, red, purple or white flowers in summer. 'Avalanche' bears white flowers and has variegated foliage. 'Kermesiana' bears red-throated fuchsia pink flowers.

Problems & Pests

Aphids and spider mites may cause problems. Check the plants carefully when purchasing.

Statice
Limonium

Height: 12–30 " **Spread:** 9–12 " **Flower color:** blue, pink, white, yellow, orange, red, purple

THIS COLORFUL PLANT is a perennial grown as an annual. It will overwinter, but it is best to start with new plants in fresh soil each season. Flowers cut from Statice keep their vivid color for weeks and combine well in bouquets with eucalyptus branches and Sunflower blooms. Statice is a forgiving plant in planters, where gardeners often forget to water regularly. If the plants look dried out, don't despair—they will come back when watered. They can be crowded into low clay bowls and will give summer color until the first frost.

Planting

Seeding: Indoors in mid-winter; direct sow in early spring

Transplanting: March through July; from six-packs

Spacing: 9–12"

Growing

Statice prefers **full sun**. The soil should be of **poor or average fertility, light, sandy** and **well drained.** The plants don't like having their roots disturbed, so if starting them indoors, use peat pots. Germination takes 14–21 days. When transplanting from six-packs, ensure you score the rootballs before planting.

Tips

Statice looks good in any sunny border, particularly in informal gardens. Although it tolerates drought and needs little maintenance, Statice will do better with summer irrigation and fertilizer. Because the stalk is sent up from the middle of the plant, the plants look better spaced closer together than is usually recommended.

Cut Statice flowers for drying late in summer once the white center has come out on the bloom. Stand them in a vase with about one inch of water, and they will dry quite nicely on their own.

Recommended

L. sinuatum forms a basal rosette of hairy leaves. The plants grow 18" tall and 12" wide, and the ridged stems bear clusters of small papery flowers in blue, purple, pink or white. '**Fortress**' has strongly branching

plants and flowers in several bright and pastel shades. The plants grow up to 24" tall. '**Pacific**' reaches a height of 24–30" and has deep rose red flowers. '**Petite Bouquet**' series has plants 12" tall and 9" wide bearing flowers in blue, purple, pink, white and yellow. '**Sunset**' grows 24" tall and bears flowers in warm red, orange, yellow, apricot and salmon shades.

Problems & Pests

Most problems can be avoided by providing a well-drained site and ensuring that there is good air circulation around the plants.

Stock
Matthiola

Height: 8–36" **Spread:** 12" **Flower color:** pink, purple, red, rose, white

STOCKS, KNOWN FOR THEIR DELIGHTFUL PERFUME, are great plants to put in your cutting bed. I am still enchanted by the memory of a bed of white stock I saw one January in front of Berkeley City Hall. Double white giants remain my favorite, although you must wait a while before they bloom.

When cutting stock flowers for arrangements, cut and then crush the woody stems so they will draw water more easily. Make sure the water in the vase is very warm.

Planting

Seeding: Indoors in mid-winter; in mild climates, direct sow in fall

Transplanting: September for winter color

Spacing: 12"

Growing

Stock plants prefer **full sun** but tolerate partial shade. The soil should be of **average fertility,** have lots of **organic matter** worked in and be **moist** but **well drained.**

Do not cover the seeds because they require light to germinate.

Tips

Stocks can be used in mixed beds or in mass plantings. Night-scented Stock should be planted where its wonderful scent can be enjoyed in the evening. It is best to plant Night-scented Stock with other plants as this stock tends to look wilted during the day, only to revive impressively at night.

Recommended

M. incana (Stock) has many cultivar groups with new ones introduced each year. Its colors range from pink and purple to red, rose or white. The height can vary from 8 to 36", depending on the cultivar. A popular cultivar is the 'Cinderella' series. The compact plants in this series grow about 10" tall and have fragrant, colorful flowers. 'Giant Mix' ('Giant Column') grows 24–36" tall and has one large spike of mostly double, lightly scented flowers per plant in shades of red, apricot, yellow, white and purple.

M. longipetala subsp. *bicornis* (Night-scented Stock, Evening-scented Stock) has pink or purple flowers that fill the evening air with their scent. The plants grow 12–18" tall. These varieties are not commonly available in nurseries. You might have more luck ordering from seed catalogs.

M. 'Starlight Scentsation' is very fragrant, growing to 18" high, with a wide range of colors. This plant does well in the border or in containers.

Problems & Pests

Poorly drained soil and low air circulation may encourage root rot or other fungal problems. Slugs may be attracted to young foliage.

Strawflower
Everlasting
Helichrysum

Height: 12–36" **Spread:** 12–18" **Flower color:** yellow, red, orange, pink, white

THERE IS A GREAT DEAL OF CONFUSION surrounding this plant, *Helichrysum bracteatum*, and the closely related *Bracteantha bracteata*. The species that appears in nurseries as a bedding plant is *Helichrysum bracteatum*, the true annual Strawflower. *Bracteantha bracteata* is a genus all its own and is considered a perennial shrub. Some references and catalogs list the two species as separate plants, some list them as being the same plant and some list one and not the other. No matter what the name, this plant is well worth growing. Strawflower combines well with Spider Flower and other low water users. I have used Strawflower in moss-lined baskets and then allowed the baskets to dry out in fall. The flowers kept their color very well over winter.

Planting

Seeding: Indoors in early spring; direct sow after last frost

Transplanting: After last frost

Spacing: 12–18"

Growing

Strawflower prefers to be planted in locations that receive **full sun**. The soil should be of **average fertility, sandy, moist** and **well drained**. Strawflower is drought tolerant. When sowing seeds, do not cover the seeds, as they require light to germinate.

Tips

Include Strawflower in mixed beds, borders and containers. The lowest growing varieties are useful edging plants. Taller varieties may require staking.

Recommended

H. bracteatum is a bushy, upright plant with medium green foliage that bears brightly colored papery flowers from summer to frost. The species can grow up to 2–3' tall and 12–18" wide, but the cultivars are generally a bit more compact. '**Dwarf Bouquet**' grows 12–15" tall and spreads 12". It produces flowers in red, yellow, pink and white.

Bracteantha bracteata is a shrub and a larger rendition of the annual

The most popular use of Strawflower is for fresh or dried flower arrangements. To dry, hang fully opened flowers upside down in bunches.

Strawflower. 'Bright Bikinis,' 'Dargan Hill Monarch' and 'Diamond Hill' are now listed under *B. bracteata*. They do not overwinter well in our Northern California winters but are effective when used as annuals.

Problems & Pests

Strawflower is susceptible to powdery mildew.

Sunflower

Helianthus

Height: dwarf varieties, 24"; giants up to 10' or more **Spread:** 12–24"
Flower color: most commonly yellow but also orange, red, brown or cream; centers are brown, purple or rusty red

SUNFLOWER has an interesting history in the United States. It is native to North America and is considered sacred by the American Indians. For a time some people considered Sunflower to be a weed, and it wasn't until the wave of Russian immigration that the plant came into its own. The plant's rapid growth, abundant seed and prized oil encouraged Russian immigrants to hybridize it to larger and larger seed-containing flowers. 'Russian Mammoth' is still the most popular Sunflower grown for food in this country. Acres of sunflowers are grown in Northern California for their oil. In the flower markets and the farmers' markets you will find outrageous colors of sunflowers used as cut flowers. 'Bright Bandolier,' 'Cinnamon Sun' and 'Prado Red' are some varieties that have no pollen to make a mess on a table.

Planting

Seeding: Indoors in late winter; direct sow in spring

Transplanting: After last frost

Spacing: 12–24"

Growing

Sunflower plants grow best in **full sun**. The soil should be of **average fertility, humus rich, moist** and **well drained**.

Sunflower plants are very popular with children and are excellent plants for them to grow. The seeds are big and easy to handle and they germinate quickly. The plants grow continually upwards, and their progress can be measured until the flower finally appears on top. If planted along the wall of a two-story house, the progress can be observed from above as well as below, making the flowers easy to see.

Tips

The lower-growing varieties can be used in beds and borders. The tall varieties are effective at the backs of borders and make good screens and temporary hedges. The tallest varieties will need staking.

Sunflower is grown as a crop seed for roasting, snacking, baking or for producing oil or flour. Use gray-seeded varieties for eating.

Birds will flock to the ripening seed-heads of your Sunflower, quickly plucking clean the tightly packed seeds. If you plan to keep the seeds to eat, you will have to place a brown paper bag or a mesh net, the sort used to keep birds out of cherry trees, around the flowerheads once the seeds set. This can be a bit of a nuisance and doesn't look too great; most gardeners leave the Sunflower's seeds to the birds and buy seeds for personal eating. Squirrels will also feed on the nutritious seeds.

Recommended

H. annuus (Common Sunflower) is considered a fairly weedy plant, but the development of many new cultivars has revived the use of this plant in the garden. '**Bright Bandolier**' bears yellow and red-brown flowers

'Teddy Bear' (this page)

on plants up to 7' tall. '**Cinnamon Sun**' grows 4–7' tall and produces cinnamon brown flowers. '**Music Box**' grows about 30" tall and has flowers in all colors, including some bicolors. '**Prado Red**' bears deep mahogany flowers, very good for cutting, on plants that grow to 5'. '**Russian Mammoth**' grows up to 10' tall or more and 24" wide and bears yellow flowers and large seeds. '**Teddy Bear**' has fuzzy-looking double flowers on plants 18–24" tall and 12–18" wide. '**Valentine**' has creamy yellow blooms with contrasting centers on plants that grow to 5'.

Problems & Pests

Powdery mildew may affect these plants.

Flowerhead going to seed (above)

Early American natives used Sunflower long before corn and beans were brought to America. They ate the seeds, ground the small kernels into flour, extracted oil from seeds for their hair and used the seeds, flower petals and pollen to make dyes for face paint, cloths and baskets.

The scientific name, Helianthus, *is from* helios *(sun) and* anthos *(flower). The face of the flower often follows the sun.*

Swan River Daisy
Brachycome

Height: 12–18" **Spread:** 12–18" **Flower color:** blue, pink, purple, white; yellow centers

I FIRST SAW THIS LONG-BLOOMING PLANT in a winery garden in Napa County. At that time, the plant had just been introduced on the market and there was not a lot of information available about it. After some digging I found the information I was after. Now the most difficult thing about it is figuring out how to pronounce the genus name. I have discovered the commonly accepted pronunciation is 'bra kihk´uh mee.' I love its many uses in planters, moss baskets, and as edging around flowerbeds. In some areas of Northern California it will overwinter, but the blooms are never the same as when first planted.

The flowers are fragrant and long lasting when cut for arrangements. Grow them in a small pot and add the pot to flower arrangements.

Planting

Seeding: Indoors in late winter; direct sow in mid-spring

Transplanting: Late spring through fall; from one-gallon cans or 4" pots

Spacing: 12–18"

Growing

Swan River Daisy prefers **full sun** but can benefit from light shade in the afternoon to prevent the plant from overheating. The soil should be **fertile** and **well drained.** Allow the soil to dry between waterings and feed the plants regularly throughout the growing season.

Transplant early because cool spring weather encourages compact, sturdy growth. This plant is frost tolerant and tends to die back when summer gets too hot. To ensure flowering into fall, cut it back about three inches as it begins to fade.

Tips

This plant works well in rock gardens, mixed containers and hanging baskets and as edging along beds. It looks good with gray-leaved plants.

Plant Swan River Daisy with plants that take longer to grow in. As Swan River Daisy is fading in July, the companions will be filling in and beginning to flower. Do not plant it in the hottest areas of the garden.

Recommended

B. iberidifolia forms a bushy, spreading mound of feathery foliage. Blue-purple or pink-purple daisy-like flowers are produced for an extended period in spring and summer. '**Bravo**' bears flowers in white, blue, purple or pink and flowers profusely in a cool but bright spot in the garden. '**Splendor**' series has dark-centered flowers in pink, purple or white.

Problems & Pests

Aphids, slugs or snails can cause trouble for this plant.

Sweet Alyssum
Lobularia

Height: 2–12" **Spread:** 6–24" **Flower color:** pink, purple, white

WHEN I PURCHASED MY BELVEDERE STORE, everyone wanted white flowers, and Sweet Alyssum has white flowers. I came to love this bedding plant and have sold hundreds of flats since. One reason it is so popular is that it can be sold in full bloom without being root-bound. Sweet Alyssum is a deterrent for whiteflies. There are several new varieties in pink, lavender and bicolor, but I still prefer the white.

The sweetness of Sweet Alyssum refers to its lovely fragrant flowers.

Planting

Seeding: Direct sow all year

Transplanting: Anytime

Spacing: 8–12"

Growing

Sweet Alyssum prefers **full sun** but tolerates light shade. Soil with **average fertility** is preferred, but poor soil is tolerated. The soil should be **moist** and **well drained.**

Sweet Alyssum plants dislike having their roots disturbed, so if starting them indoors, use peat pots or pellets. Sweet Alyssum flowers very quickly from seed. Trim Sweet Alyssum back occasionally over summer to keep it flowering and looking good.

Tips

Sweet Alyssum will creep around rock gardens, on rock walls, between paving stones and along the edges of beds. It can fill in the spaces between taller plants in borders and mixed containers.

Leave Sweet Alyssum to sit out all winter. In spring, remove the previous year's plant to expose self-sown seedlings below.

Recommended

L. maritima forms a low, spreading mound of foliage. The plant appears to be covered in blossoms when it is in full flower. 'Rosie O'Day' bears rose pink to lavender pink flowers on 2–4" tall, wide-spreading plants. 'Snow Crystal' grows to 10" tall and bears large, bright white flowers profusely all summer. 'Wonderland'

series has a mix of all colors including apricot, lavender, rose, purple and white on compact plants 6" tall.

Problems & Pests

Sweet Alyssum rarely has any problems but is sometimes afflicted with downy mildew, slugs and snails. It is so easy to grow that if any problems arise, pull out the old plants and put in new ones if needed.

'Wonderland' (below)

Sweet Pea
Lathyrus

Height: up to 6'; bush varieties about 2–36" **Spread:** 12–36"
Flower color: pink, red, purple, lavender, blue, salmon, pale yellow, peach, white or bicolored

SWEET PEAS ARE WONDERFUL cool-weather annuals either for climbing or as a bush. Climbing Sweet Peas will have more picking flowers, but the bush varieties do better as landscape or container plants. In Northern California Sweet Peas are considered winter- and spring-blooming plants. They are best planted in fall when there is still warm enough weather to allow the seeds to germinate. They don't transplant well, although I have had some modest success growing the bush type in containers from six-packs. Follow the procedure in the Growing section on the next page, and from January to the end of April you will be blessed with copious fragrant picking blooms.

Planting

Seeding: Direct sow in October; see below

Spacing: 6–36"

Growing

To grow Sweet Peas successfully in Northern California takes some special measures. Dig a trench one foot deep and one shovel-width wide. Mix equal parts of blood meal, bone meal and alfalfa meal with half of the excavated soil. Use about one pound of fertilizer for every 20 feet of row length. Fill the bottom six inches of the trench with the soil/fertilizer mix. Mix the remaining soil with equal parts of planting mix. Add a one-inch layer of this 50/50 mix into the trench.

Soak the Sweet Pea seeds overnight in warm water and plant them in the trench three inches apart. Cover the row with a row cover to prevent birds, especially migrating sparrows, from eating the freshly sprouted seeds.

As the seeds germinate, cover them with the prepared 50/50 mix. Backfill as the seedlings push themselves towards the top of the trench. The process takes about four weeks, until the plants reach the top of the trench. They then need a trellis to grow on. Thin seedlings to six inches apart when they reach the true leaf stage.

Once the Sweet Peas are up and growing, problems are minimal. In May they will start to look sick, and that is a good time to replace them with something else.

Sweet Peas are attractive and long lasting as cut flowers. The more Sweet Pea flowers you cut, the more the plant will bloom.

This planting and growing process is a lot of effort, but it is well worth it.

Sweet Peas prefer **full sun** but tolerate light shade. The soil should be **fertile**, high in **organic matter, moist** and **well drained**. The plants will tolerate light frost. Remove all spent flowers.

Tips

Sweet Peas will grow up poles, trellises and fences or over rocks. The low-growing varieties will form low, shrubby mounds. An excellent way to provide privacy and hide a chain-link fence is to grow Sweet Peas up it.

To help prevent some diseases from afflicting your Sweet Peas, avoid planting Sweet Peas in the same location two years in a row.

Fertilize very lightly during flowering season.

Recommended

Many cultivars of *L. odoratus* are available. '**Bijou**' series is a popular heat-resistant variety that grows 12–18" tall, with an equal spread. It needs no support to grow. '**Bouquet**' mixed is a tall, climbing variety. '**Cupid**' grows 2–4" tall and trails to 12" with flowers in a wide range of colors. '**Knee Hi**' plants are bushy and grow 24–36" tall. Plants in this group will need some support. A peony or tomato cage works very well, or insert a twiggy branch that the stems can grow through. Flowers in this group come in shades of red, pink, white and blue. '**Mammoth Mix**' has early spring flowers in shades of pink, blue, red, purple and rose. This climber will need support. **'Supersnoop'** series is a sturdy bush type that needs no support, growing 24" tall and 36" wide. The plant is fragrant with long stems. Pinch its tips to encourage low growth.

Problems & Pests

Slugs and snails may eat the foliage of young plants. Root rot, mildew, rust and leaf spot may also afflict Sweet Peas occasionally. A preventive spray with compost tea or fish emulsion should avert the fungal disease problems.

Sweet Potato Vine

Ipomoea

Height: 4–30' **Spread:** 12–24" **Flower color:** white, blue, pink, purple and variegated

LIME-COLORED 'MARGUERITE' is exceptional when used in planters with red Ivy-leaved Geranium and plants with gray foliage, such as Dusty Miller. I know the cultivars of Sweet Potato Vine set a tuber, but I have never had the courage to eat them. For eating I grow the species *(Ipomoea batatas)* that I know is the real thing and not ornamental. My uncle used Moonflower as a lanai cover at his home in Sacramento along with some grapevines. He was always telling the more gullible of us that this vine was the only blooming grapevine in the country.

I. batatas, *Sweet Potato Vine, is best recognized by the large lime green, heart-shaped leaves, but it is also available in shades of purple.*

Planting

Seeding: Indoors in early spring; direct sow after last frost

Transplanting: Late spring

Spacing: 12–18"

Growing

Grow sweet potato vines in **full sun.** The plants prefer a **light, well-drained** soil with **poor to moderate fertility.** Before sowing, soak seeds for 24 hours and/or notch the seed coating with a file. If starting seeds indoors, use peat pots.

I. batatas cultivar (above)

Tips

Sweet potato vines are effective in containers and hanging baskets. These cascading plants can also be trained to grow up a trellis. As groundcovers, they will grow over any obstacles they encounter, rooting where the stems contact the ground. If you have a sunny window, consider starting a hanging basket of sweet potato vine indoors for a unique winter display. Train the vines to grow up around the hangers and then let them spill over the sides of the pot, providing nice foliage and flowers.

The twining selections can be grown over trellises, arbors, iron or chain-link fences or any place you would like to cover. They must twine around objects in order to climb them. Wide fence posts, walls or other broad objects must have a trellis or some wire or twine attached to them to provide the vines with something to grow up.

'Marguerite' with petunias and zinnias (right)

'Blackie' with English Ivy (above)

'Blackie' (center), 'Marguerite' (below)

Each flower of an *Ipomoea* plant lasts for only one day. The buds form a spiral that slowly unfurls as the day brightens with the rising sun (except *I. alba*, whose flowers open at night.)

I. nil and *I. tricolor* should be removed during fall cleanup. Both re-seed. Remove any you don't want and allow others to grow.

Recommended

I. batatas (Sweet Potato Vine) has trailing stems to 20' and bears pale pink, pale purple, rose-purple or lavender flowers in summer. Originally grown for the tubers that form on the roots, this plant has recently become popular for its attractive foliage. **'Blackie'** has dark purple, almost black, deeply lobed leaves. **'Marguerite'** ('Terrace Lime') has pale lime green foliage on a fairly compact plant. Both these cultivars reach 4–6' in length.

Alternate Species

I. alba (Moonflower) bears large white flowers that open at night or on cloudy or dark days. The vine quickly grows 15–30' tall and is readily available from seed. This plant is ideal for hot areas in Northern California, because heat is a major requirement for its success. It combines well with other annual vines such as Scarlet Runner Bean and Hyacinth Bean. It has a wonderful fragrance on hot summer evenings.

I. lobata (Mina Lobata, Firecracker Vine, Exotic Love) is a twining climber growing 6–15'. The flowers are borne along one side of a spike. The buds are red, and the flowers are orange fading to yellow, giving the spike a fire-like appearance.

I. x *multifida (I.* x *sloteri)* (Cardinal Climber) is a twining climber growing 6–10'. It has deeply lobed leaves and bears white-throated red flowers in summer.

I. nil is a vigorous climber growing 15' or more. The white-throated flowers in shades of blue, red or purple bloom in summer. Flowers may also come in shades of red and purple. '**Chocolate**' bears red-tinged, chocolate brown flowers. Early-blooming '**Early Call**' produces white-throated scarlet flowers.

I. quamoclit (Cypress Vine) is a twining climber that grows 6–20' tall and bears scarlet red flowers in summer. The plant is not well known but is now locally available by seed.

I. tricolor (Morning Glory) is a vigorous, twining vine reaching 10–15'. The flowers, which open with the rise of the sun, are blue with a white throat. There are several cultivars including '**Heavenly Blue**,' with white-centered, sky blue flowers. Other cultivars produce pink, blue, lavender, red and white flowers with contrasting throats in singles, doubles and bicolors.

Grow I. alba, *Moonflower, on a porch or on a trellis near a patio that is used in the evenings, so the sweetly scented flowers can be fully enjoyed.*

I. tricolor (above & center)

I. alba (below)

Sweet William
Dianthus

Height: 6–30" **Spread:** 8–12" **Flower color:** white, pink, red, purple

SWEET WILLIAMS are wonderful when combined with other *Dianthus* varieties such as Clove Pink. Many of the *Dianthus* varieties combine well with each other, but their vivid color is somewhat difficult to blend with annuals such as marigolds or zinnias. The dwarf cultivars such as 'Indian Carpet' are beautiful in moss baskets and can add color when planted into more permanent hanging baskets. A lot of people use ivy or Vinca minor in their hanging baskets. Adding sweet Williams will give these baskets an attractive splash of color. It is a good idea to feed these baskets with liquid fertilizers twice a month to keep them at their best.

Planting

Seeding: Sow seed in late spring to early summer for bloom the following year; sow seed of *D. chinensis* in fall or indoors in spring

Transplanting: Spring

Spacing: 6–12"

Growing

Sweet Williams prefer **full sun** but tolerate some light shade. A **light, neutral or alkaline, humus-rich, well-drained** soil is preferred. The most important factor in the successful cultivation of sweet Williams is drainage. Mix organic matter into their area of the flowerbed to encourage good drainage. Growing these plants in slightly alkaline soil will produce excellent color over a long period.

Deadhead as the flowers fade to prolong blooming. Leave a few flowers in place to go to seed, and the plants will self-seed quite easily. Seedlings may differ from the parent plants, often with new and interesting results.

Tips

Sweet Williams are great for mass planting in the rock garden, and for edging flower borders and walkways. Try these plants for cut flowers.

Keep sheltered from strong winds and the hottest afternoon sun.

Recommended

D. barbatus (Sweet William) is a biennial mostly grown as an annual. It reaches a height of 18–24" tall and spreads 8–12". Flattened clusters of

'Telstar Crimson' (above)

The tiny, delicate petals of pinks can be used to decorate cakes. Be sure to remove the bitter white part at the base of each petal before using the petals.

often two-toned white, pink, red or purple-red flowers bloom in late spring to early summer. 'Hollandia Mix' grows to 30" tall. The compact 'Indian Carpet' grows 6–8" tall. 'Roundabout' series grows 8–12" tall and produces solid or two-toned blooms in the first year from seed. 'Summer Beauty' reaches a height of 12".

Alternate Species

D. caryophyllus (Wild Carnation, Clove Pink) has been cultivated for centuries and is the ancestor of today's many border carnations and florist (perpetual flowering) carnations. Most selections have double flowers with a prominent, spicy-sweet fragrance and come in almost all colors except true blue. Florist carnations are perennial and belong in hothouse conditions. Border carnations are also perennials but are best treated as annuals. They are smaller, bushy plants that grow 6–14" tall and sometimes taller. 'Cinnamon Red Hots' produces vivid red flowers on 12" tall plants. 'Pinkie' grows 6–12" tall and bears rose pink flowers. 'Pixie Delight' grows 12–18" tall with flowers in a wide range of colors. Check with your local nursery or garden center to see what is available. There are thousands of named cultivars and varieties.

D. chinensis (China Pink, Annual Pink) is an erect, mound-forming plant growing 6–30" tall and 8–12" wide. The fragrant flowers come in pink, red, white and light purple and are produced for an extended period in late spring and summer. Many cultivars are available. The 'Telstar'

series are hybrids of *D. chinensis* and *D. barbatus* and are usually listed under *D. chinensis*. They grow 8–12" tall and wide, producing blooms in shades of pink, red and white in solid and two-toned forms.

D. 'Rainbow Loveliness' grows to 24" tall and bears very fragrant flowers in shades of white, pink and lavender.

Problems & Pests

Rust and fusarium wilt may be problems. Providing good drainage and air circulation will keep most fungal problems away. Occasional problems with slugs, snails and sow bugs are possible.

D. barbatus (above), 'Telstar Pink' (below)

The genus name, Dianthus, *is a combination of* Dios *(a form of the name Zeus) and* anthos *(flower), so means 'flower of the gods.' There are more than 300 annual and perennial species and varieties in this genus.*

Transvaal Daisy
Gerbera Daisy
Gerbera

Height: 8–24" **Spread**: up to 24" **Flower color**: pink, purple, red, orange, yellow

I FIRST SAW A TRANSVAAL DAISY bloom in a florist box with only the flower showing. I thought at the time that it would be wonderful if nature could create such perfection. I was floored when I later found out it was an actually living plant! When Transvaal Daisy first came on the market 30 years ago, the plants had to be staked. There are now many varieties sturdy enough to not need staking. The colors lend themselves to be planted with a Lobelia border, but Transvaal Daisy plants are best when they stand alone in the flowerbed.

Planting

Seeding: Not recommended; basal cuttings can be taken in summer

Transplanting: March through April; best from 4" pots but also available in six-packs

Spacing: 18–24"

Growing

Transvaal Daisy prefers **full sun** but tolerates partial shade. The soil should be **well drained,** have plenty of **organic matter** worked in and be of **average to high fertility**. To keep the crown of the plant dry, set the crown just above the soil line. If your soil is poorly drained, use a raised bed. Allow soil to almost dry out between waterings.

Transvaal Daisy prefers warm weather. Regular watering and feeding is a must. In the Sacramento Valley and other hot spots in California, this plant needs shade from the hot afternoon sun.

Transvaal Daisy can be quite difficult to grow from seed. It is easier to purchase plants in spring. If you are a glutton for punishment and want to attempt to grow the plants from seed, use only very fresh seed, because the seeds lose viability very quickly. When seeding indoors, start them in December or January and cover the seed flat or pot with clear plastic to maintain high humidity while the seeds are germinating. When transplanting, be careful not to plant too deeply.

Tips

Transvaal Daisy makes an impressive addition to annual beds and borders as well as in mixed or solo containers.

Transvaal Daisy is popular as a cut flower. For longer lasting flowers, slit the bottoms of the stems up one inch to help them absorb water. Do this cut under warm water for maximum water saturation in the stem.

Recommended

G. jamesonii is a clump-forming plant 12–18" tall and 24" wide. Yellow-centered flowers in solid shades of yellow, orange, apricot and red

Transvaal Daisy is also popular as a short-lived houseplant.

bloom from late spring to late summer. **'California Giants'** grows to 24" tall, with flowers in red, orange, yellow and pink. **'Happipot'** has compact plants that grow to 8" tall, with mixed flower colors. **'Skipper'** has smaller leaves and shorter stems and grows 8–10" tall. It is good for edging beds or for containers.

Problems & Pests

Slugs and snails, crown rot and root rot are the most common problems. Leaf miners, aphids, thrips and whiteflies can also be troublesome. Watch out for powdery mildew in very moist regions of the Bay Area.

Verbena
Garden Verbena, Vervain
Verbena

Height: 3"–6' **Spread:** 12–36" **Flower color:** red, pink, purple, yellow, peach, blue, white; usually white centers

LIFE USED TO BE SIMPLE. There were two verbenas, one variety of pansy, three salvias, and I knew them all by their first names. Hybridizers have had a wonderful time crossing one variety with another to form more varieties than anyone has room for in one garden. Some of my favorites are 'Peaches and Cream,' 'Homestead Purple,' Tapien Hybrids and Temari Hybrids. The latter two are constantly being added to with different colors. I have one comment about mixing colors in the garden: God doesn't mind. Take a look at the prairies in the Midwest, where shades of orange, red, pink and purple combine in the most outrageous combinations to make a wonderful blanket of color.

Verbenas have been known since ancient times. When the Romans sent messengers of peace to other nations, they adorned their apparel with sprays of verbena.

Planting

Seeding: Indoors in mid-winter

Transplanting: After last frost; best from six-packs

Spacing: 18"

Growing

Verbenas grow best in **full sun**. The soil should be **fertile** and **very well drained** although most plants will grow in average to heavy soils. They will benefit from a mulch added during the summer growing season.

Verbenas are among those perennials best treated as annuals. Moisten the soil before sowing seeds. Chill seeds one week before sowing. Do not cover the seeds with soil. Place the entire seed tray or pots in darkness, or cover with newspaper or black plastic until seeds germinate. Water the seeds only if the soil becomes very dry. Once seeds germinate, they can be moved into the light.

Pinch back young plants to promote bushy growth.

V. x hybrida (this page)

For fall blooms, cut back the plants to half their size in mid-summer.

V. bonariensis (this page)

Tips

Their bright colors and tolerance of dry locations make verbenas useful on rock walls and in beds, borders, rock gardens, containers, hanging baskets and window boxes. Many of the lower-growing plants are good substitutes for ivy geraniums when planted where the sun is hot and where a roof overhang keeps these mildew-prone plants dry.

Recommended

V. bonariensis forms a low clump of foliage from which tall, stiff, flower-bearing stems emerge. The small purple flowers are held in clusters and make one of the best cut flowers for fresh or dry arrangements. This plant grows 36–72" tall and 18–36" wide. This species may survive a mild winter but will likely look ratty the next year. Pull these plants out each fall. Don't worry about replanting— the plants will re-seed.

V. '**Homestead Purple**' is a mildew-resistant selection. It has shiny, dark green foliage and bears deep purple flowers in summer. It grows 12–24" tall and spreads up to 36" wide.

V. x hybrida is a bushy plant that may be upright or spreading. It grows 6–12" tall and 18–36" wide and bears clusters of small flowers in shades of white, purple, blue, pink, red or yellow. '**Peaches and Cream**' is a spreading plant with flowers that open to a soft peach color and fade to white. '**Romance**' series has red, pink, purple or white flowers, with white eyes on plants 6–10" tall. '**Showtime**' bears brightly colored flowers on compact plants that grow to 10" tall and spread 18". *V.* x *hybrida* selections are often used as groundcovers. They are ideal for borders and as fillers around taller annuals and perennials.

V. **Tapien Hybrids** are low-growing perennials grown as annuals. They have dissected leaves and grow 4" tall and 12–18" wide. Summer flowers bloom in shades of purple, pink, red and blue. New introductions of colors come on the market annually.

V. **Temari Hybrids** are also low-growing perennials grown as annuals. They reach a height of 3" and a spread of 24–30". They have wide, dark green foliage and bear flowers of bright pink, purple and burgundy in summer.

Tapien Hybrids (above), *V. bonariensis* with impatiens and petunias (below)

Problems & Pests

Aphids, whiteflies, slugs and snails may be troublesome. Avoid fungal problems, especially in wet climates, by making sure there is good air circulation around the plant and that the soil is well drained.

The Verbena *genus consists of about 200 hardy and tender perennials, some of which are semi-evergreen. They are natives of North and South America.*

Vinca Rosea
Madagascar Periwinkle
Catharanthus (Vinca)

Height: 12–24" **Spread:** usually equal to or greater than height
Flower color: red, pink, white; often with contrasting centers

VINCA ROSEA takes over where Busy Lizzie Impatiens wilts in the sun.
Because the two plants look similar, using them together can provide landscape continuity from shade to sun. Vinca Rosea likes heat. Where summers
are cool, you need to keep flowerbeds on the dry side to keep the soil temperature at its highest.

Planting

Seeding: Indoors in mid-winter

Transplanting: After last frost

Spacing: 8–18"

Growing

Vinca Rosea prefers full sun but tolerates partial shade. **Any soil** is fine. This plant tolerates pollution and drought but prefers to be watered regularly, and it doesn't like to be too wet or too cold.

Keep seedlings warm and take care not to overwater them. The soil temperature should be 55–64° F for seeds to germinate.

Tips

Vinca Rosea does well in the sunniest, warmest part of the garden. Plant in a bed along an exposed driveway or against the south-facing wall of the house. It can also be used in hanging baskets, planters and as a temporary groundcover.

Vinca Rosea is a perennial that is grown as an annual. In a bright room, it can be grown as a houseplant. It is easily grown from cuttings.

Recommended

C. roseus (*Vinca rosea*) forms a mound of strong stems. The plants grow 12–24" tall, with an equal spread. The plant blooms for an extended period in summer and into fall in mild weather, and the flowers are pink, red or white, often with contrasting centers. **'Apricot Delight'** bears pale apricot flowers with bright raspberry red centers.

'Cooler' series has light-colored flowers with darker, contrasting centers. **'Pacifica'** has flowers in various colors on compact plants.

Problems & Pests

Slugs can be troublesome. Most rot and fungal problems can be avoided by not overwatering the plants.

Viola

Viola

Height: 6–12" **Spread:** 6–12" **Flower color:** blue, purple, red, orange, yellow, pink, white, black or multi-colored

THESE WONDERFUL winter and spring bloomers are beautiful, although I've been looking for the faces in viola and pansy flowers for years with no luck. Violas are my favorite flowers for short mass plantings. They have shorter stems than pansies and hold their heads high even after a heavy rain. One year in my large flowerbed in Belvedere, I planted red and white pansies. I am a graduate of the University of California at Berkeley, whose school colors are blue and gold, and when the Stanford graduates noticed the red and white pansies, they thought that I was honoring their alma mater and Cal's archenemy. But when the bed came into full bloom and spelled out 'GO BEARS,' my support for Cal's Golden Bears was clear.

Planting

Seeding: Indoors in early winter or mid-summer

Transplanting: Anytime

Spacing: 6"

Growing

Violas prefer **full sun** but tolerate partial shade. The soil should be **fertile, moist** and **well drained**.

Direct sowing is not recommended. Sow seeds indoors in early winter for spring flowers and in mid-summer for fall and early-winter blooms. Germination will be greater if seeds are kept in darkness until they germinate. Place seed trays in a dark closet or cover with dark plastic or layers of newspaper to provide enough darkness.

V. tricolor (above), *V.* x *wittrockiana* (below)

Violas do well when the weather is cool. They may even die back completely in summer. Plants may rejuvenate in fall, but it is often easier to plant new ones at that time, so as not to take up summer garden space with plants that don't look very good.

In the interior valley areas, violas can be planted in full sun from October through February. During warmer weather, it is best to plant them in an area that will receive sun in the morning only.

Tips

The color combinations for both violas and pansies are astounding. Violas can be used in beds, borders, and in mixed plantings with spring-flowering bulbs. They combine well with other plants in containers and moss-lined hanging baskets.

V. x *wittrockiana* (this page)

The large-flowering violas combine well with primroses in garden beds for early-spring color and in hanging baskets for winter color. For something unusual and edible, add some loose-leaf lettuce to the basket.

Violas survive temperatures to 20° F. To get the colors you want, purchase them in bloom. Remove all buds and flowers and score the roots before planting. Violas are very rugged plants that don't require delicate handling.

Recommended

V. tricolor (Johnny-jump-up) is a popular species growing 6–12" tall and wide. The flowers are purple, white and yellow, usually in combination, although several varieties have flowers in a single color, often purple. This plant will thrive in gravel. **'Bowles Black'** has dark purple flowers that appear to be almost black. The center of each flower is yellow. **'Helen Mount'** ('Helen Mound') bears large flowers in the traditional purple, yellow and white combination. Plants in the **'Sorbet'** series are compact and produce purple-centered, black-and-white flowers. **'Splendid'** series has larger, rounder flowers than other *V. tricolor* selections on dwarf, creeping plants that spread about 12".

V. x *wittrockiana* (Pansy) comes in blue, purple, red, orange, yellow, pink and white, often multi-colored or with face-like markings. The plants form clumps 6–10" tall and 9–12" wide. **'Crystal Bowl'** bears flowers in clear, solid colors. **'Floral Dance'** has flowers in a variety of solid colors and multi-colors. It is popular for spring and fall displays as it is cold hardy. 'Imperial' series bears large flowers in a good range of unique colors. 'Imperial Frosty Rose' has flowers with deep rose pink centers that gradually pale to white near the edges of the petals. 'Joker' series has bicolored or multi-colored flowers with distinctive face markings. The flowers come in all colors. 'Maxim Marina' bears light blue flowers with white-rimmed dark blue blotches at the center. This cultivar tolerates both hot and cold temperatures. 'Watercolor' series is a newer group of cultivars with flowers in delicate pastel shades.

V. x wittrockiana (this page), with tulips (below)

Problems & Pests

Slugs and snails can be problems. Avoid fungal problems by ensuring good air circulation and good drainage.

Collect short vases, such as perfume bottles with narrow necks, for displaying the cut flowers of violas. The more you pick, the more profusely the plants will bloom. These flowers are also easy to press between sheets of wax paper weighted down with books.

Wishbone Flower
Torenia

Height: 6–12" **Spread:** 6–12" **Flower color:** purple, blue, white; often bicolored with yellow spot on lower petal

ONE OF THE SECRETS of growing this plant is perfect drainage. It is sensitive to root rot if allowed to stand in puddles of water for an extended time. In the Sacramento Valley, Wishbone Flower will need shade from the hot afternoon sun. In some parts of the coast the plants will re-seed themselves when their environment makes them happy. They can add an unusual flair to moss baskets when combined with violas, Sweet Alyssum and *Lobelia* 'Cambridge Blue.'

Planting

Seeding: Indoors in mid-winter

Transplanting: After last frost

Spacing: 8"

Growing

Wishbone Flower prefers to grow in **full sun,** providing there is afternoon shade in the hottest areas. The soil should be **fertile, light,** rich in **organic matter** and **moist.** This plant needs to be watered and fed regularly. If planted in full sun, it is a good idea to use an organic mulch to keep the roots cool.

Don't cover the seeds when planting as they need light to germinate.

Tips

Wishbone Flower can be massed in a bed or border, used as an edging plant and mixed with other plants in containers or hanging baskets. It can also be grown as a houseplant.

The appearance of this plant is very soothing and subtle, allowing it to blend well with other flowers in the garden.

Recommended

T. fournieri is an upright, mounding plant. It bears yellow-throated, purple-blue flowers all summer and often into fall. It grows about 12" tall and wide. 'Alba' bears white flowers. 'Clown' series has compact plants, 6–8" tall, with early blooms in all colors.

Problems & Pests

Some fungal problems may develop if the soil is too wet. Although it likes moist soil, it also requires good air circulation around its roots. Overwatering and poor drainage may damage the plant.

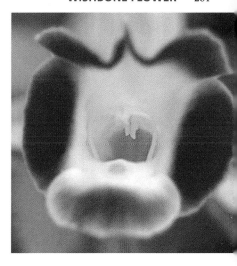

The name Wishbone Flower comes from the fact that the stamens look like small wishbones. Put the plants in a place where you can see the inside of the flowers.

Zinnia
Zinnia

Height: 6–36" **Spread:** 14–24" **Flower color:** red, yellow, green, purple, orange, pink, white

ZINNIAS are one of the greatest flowers to add to a cut-flower garden. On the other hand, don't overlook the smaller varieties that can make colorful borders. Powdery mildew is a problem where it's foggy in such areas as San Francisco, Marin County and Mendocino County. Water in the early morning, before 10 o'clock, to allow the foliage to dry before evening. If powdery mildew appears, spray with horticultural oil to protect the foliage. However, once zinnias suffer mildew it is best to replace them with varieties of annuals that are not susceptible to mildew. They are low water users and combine well with other low water users such as salvias, Sunflower and coreopsis.

Planting

Seeding: Indoors in late winter; direct sow after last frost

Transplanting: After last frost

Spacing: 6–12"

Growing

Zinnias grow best in **full sun.** The soil should be **fertile,** rich in **organic matter, moist** and **well drained.**

When starting the seeds indoors, plant them in individual peat pots to avoid disturbing the roots when transplanting.

'Profusion White' (above), 'Classic' (below)

These pretty annuals are natives of Mexico.

Tips

Zinnias are useful in beds and borders, in containers and in cutting gardens. The dwarf varieties can be used as edging plants. They are great for fall color. Combine the rounded form of the zinnia flower with the spiky blooms of a salvia, or use the taller varieties in front of Sunflower plants in fertile soil in a dry, sunny location both plants will love.

Deadhead zinnias to keep them flowering and looking their best. To keep mildew from the leaves, plant mildew-resistant varieties and avoid wetting the foliage when you water.

Recommended

Z. angustifolia is an erect plant growing 14–16" tall and wide. It has narrow leaves and bears bright orange flowers. The center of the flowers are orange with black or deep purple and each flower petal has a yellow stripe up the middle.

'Classic' grows 10–12" tall and spreads up to 24" wide, producing tangerine orange flowers. It grows and blooms quickly from seed and flowers well into fall. Use it where you wish to fill in areas that just need a little something to brighten the landscape. It is ideal for hanging baskets in full sun. This plant is self-grooming and disease-free.

Z. elegans (Common Zinnia) flowers come in several forms including single, double and cactus flowered. On a cactus-flowered bloom the petals appear to be rolled into tubes like the quills of a cactus. **'California Giants'** has large double flowers in a wide range of colors. The bushy plants grow to 36" tall. **'Peter Pan'** grows up to 12" tall, but it starts blooming early at 6", with flowers in mixed colors. **'Thumbelina'** series has small flowers in all colors on dwarf,

'California Giants' (below)

6" plants. This selection tolerates wet weather better than most zinnias.

Z. 'Profusion' is a fast-growing, mildew-resistant hybrid. It has flowers in orange, red or white on compact plants that grow 10–12" tall.

Problems & Pests

Zinnias are prone to mildew and other fungal problems. Prevent such problems by ensuring good air circulation and drainage.

Though zinnias are quite drought tolerant, they will grow best if watered thoroughly when their soil dries out. Use a soaker hose to avoid wetting the leaves.

Zinnias make excellent, long-lasting cut flowers for fresh arrangements.

HEIGHT LEGEND: Low: < 12" • Medium: 12–24" • Tall: > 24"

SPECIES
by Common Name

	COLOR									SOWING		HEIGHT		
	White	Pink	Red	Orange	Yellow	Blue	Purple	Green	Foliage	Indoors	Direct	Low	Medium	Tall
African Daisy	*	*	*	*	*					*	*		*	
Ageratum	*	*				*	*			*	*	*	*	
Amaranth			*		*			*		*	*			*
Amethyst Flower	*					*	*				*	*	*	
Angelica	*				*		*			*	*			*
Baby's Breath	*	*					*			*	*		*	*
Bachelor's Buttons	*	*	*			*	*			*	*		*	*
Bacopa	*						*					*		
Begonia	*	*	*	*	*					*		*		
Bells-of-Ireland								*		*	*		*	*
Bird's Eyes						*					*	*		
Black-eyed Susan			*	*	*					*	*		*	*
Black-eyed Susan Vine	*			*	*					*	*			*
Blanket Flower			*	*	*					*	*		*	*
Blue Lace Flower	*					*					*	*		
Butterfly Weed			*	*	*					*			*	*
California Poppy		*	*	*	*						*	*	*	
Candytuft	*	*	*				*			*	*	*	*	
Canterbury Bells	*	*				*	*			*	*		*	*
Cape Marigold	*	*		*	*					*	*		*	
Cathedral Bells	*						*			*				*
Chickabiddy	*	*	*			*	*			*				*
China Aster	*	*	*	*	*	*	*			*	*	*	*	*
Chinese Forget-me-not						*				*	*		*	
Coleus							*		*	*		*	*	
Coreopsis			*	*	*					*	*	*	*	*
Corn Cockle	*	*					*				*			*
Cosmos	*	*	*	*	*					*	*		*	*
Creeping Zinnia				*	*						*	*		

Hardy	Half-hardy	Tender	Sun	Part Shade	Light Shade	Shade	Moist	Well Drained	Dry	Fertile	Average	Poor	Page Number	SPECIES by Common Name
		*	*				*	*			*		50	African Daisy
	*		*	*			*	*		*			52	Ageratum
		*	*					*			*	*	56	Amaranth
		*		*	*	*		*		*			60	Amethyst Flower
	*		*	*			*			*			62	Angelica
*			*					*				*	64	Baby's Breath
*			*				*			*	*		68	Bachelor's Buttons
		*	*	*			*	*			*		70	Bacopa
		*		*	*	*		*		*			72	Begonia
	*		*	*			*	*		*	*		74	Bells-of-Ireland
*			*					*			*	*	76	Bird's Eyes
*			*	*			*	*			*		78	Black-eyed Susan
		*	*	*	*		*	*		*			82	Black-eyed Susan Vine
*			*					*			*	*	84	Blanket Flower
*			*					*			*		86	Blue Lace Flower
*			*					*			*	*	88	Butterfly Weed
*			*	*				*			*	*	90	California Poppy
*			*					*			*	*	94	Candytuft
*			*	*			*	*		*			96	Canterbury Bells
		*	*					*		*			100	Cape Marigold
		*	*					*			*		102	Cathedral Bells
		*		*	*			*		*			104	Chickabiddy
		*	*	*			*	*		*			106	China Aster
*				*	*	*	*	*			*		108	Chinese Forget-me-not
	*		*	*	*	*	*	*		*	*		110	Coleus
*			*					*		*	*		114	Coreopsis
*			*					*			*	*	118	Corn Cockle
	*		*					*			*	*	120	Cosmos
	*		*					*			*		124	Creeping Zinnia

HEIGHT LEGEND: Low: < 12" • Medium: 12–24" • Tall: > 24"

SPECIES by Common Name	COLOR									SOWING		HEIGHT		
	White	Pink	Red	Orange	Yellow	Blue	Purple	Green	Foliage	Indoors	Direct	Low	Medium	Tall
Cup Flower	*					*	*			*	*	*		
Dahlia	*	*	*	*	*		*			*	*	*	*	
Diascia		*								*		*		
English Daisy	*	*	*							*	*	*		
Flowering Maple	*	*	*	*	*					*	*			*
Flowering Tobacco	*	*	*				*	*		*	*		*	*
Forget-me-not	*	*				*					*	*		
Fried-egg Flower	*				*						*	*		
Geranium	*	*	*	*			*			*	*	*	*	
Globe Amaranth	*	*	*				*			*		*	*	*
Godetia	*	*	*				*				*		*	*
Heliotrope	*						*			*		*	*	
Hollyhock	*	*	*		*		*			*	*			*
Impatiens	*	*	*	*			*			*		*	*	*
Larkspur	*	*				*	*			*	*		*	*
Lobelia	*	*	*			*	*			*		*		
Love-in-a-mist	*	*				*	*			*	*		*	
Lychnis	*	*	*								*			*
Mallow	*	*	*							*	*			*
Marigold			*	*	*					*	*	*	*	*
Mexican Sunflower			*	*	*					*	*			*
Million Bells	*	*	*	*	*	*	*					*		
Moss Rose	*	*	*	*	*		*			*		*		
Nasturtium	*	*	*	*	*						*	*	*	
Nemesia	*	*	*	*	*	*	*			*		*		
Ornamental Kale									*		*		*	
Painted Daisy	*	*	*		*		*			*	*	*	*	*
Painted-Tongue		*	*	*	*	*	*			*				*
Petunia	*	*	*		*		*			*		*	*	

Hardy	Half-hardy	Tender	Sun	Part Shade	Light Shade	Shade	Moist	Well Drained	Dry	Fertile	Average	Poor	Page Number	SPECIES by Common Name
	*		*	*			*	*		*			126	Cup Flower
		*	*				*	*		*			128	Dahlia
	*		*				*	*		*			132	Diascia
	*		*	*	*		*			*	*		134	English Daisy
		*	*					*			*		136	Flowering Maple
		*	*	*	*		*	*		*			140	Flowering Tobacco
*				*	*		*	*		*			144	Forget-me-not
*			*	*			*	*		*			146	Fried-egg Flower
		*	*	*				*		*			148	Geranium
		*	*					*			*		152	Globe Amaranth
*			*		*			*	*		*	*	154	Godetia
		*	*				*	*		*			156	Heliotrope
*	*		*	*				*			*	*	158	Hollyhock
		*	*	*	*	*	*	*		*			160	Impatiens
*			*		*			*		*			164	Larkspur
*			*	*			*	*		*			166	Lobelia
*			*	*			*	*			*		168	Love-in-a-mist
*			*	*			*	*			*		170	Lychnis
*			*					*			*		174	Mallow
	*		*					*	*		*		178	Marigold
		*	*					*	*		*	*	182	Mexican Sunflower
	*		*	*	*		*	*		*			184	Million Bells
		*	*					*	*			*	186	Moss Rose
		*	*	*				*			*	*	188	Nasturtium
	*		*				*	*		*			192	Nemesia
*			*	*			*	*		*			194	Ornamental Kale
*			*	*				*			*		198	Painted Daisy
		*	*				*	*		*			200	Painted-Tongue
	*		*					*			*	*	202	Petunia

HEIGHT LEGEND: Low: < 12" • Medium: 12–24" • Tall: > 24"

SPECIES by Common Name	White	Pink	Red	Orange	Yellow	Blue	Purple	Green	Foliage	Indoors	Direct	Low	Medium	Tall
Phlox	*	*	*		*	*	*			*	*	*	*	
Pincushion Flower	*	*	*			*	*			*	*		*	*
Poor Man's Orchid	*	*	*	*	*		*			*	*	*	*	
Poppy	*	*	*	*	*		*				*	*	*	*
Pot Marigold				*	*						*	*	*	
Prickly Poppy				*	*					*	*			*
Rock Cress	*	*								*		*		
Salvia	*	*	*	*			*	*		*	*		*	*
Scarlet Runner Bean			*								*			*
Snapdragon	*	*	*	*	*		*			*	*		*	*
Spider Flower	*	*	*				*			*	*			*
Star Clusters	*	*	*				*			*	*			*
Statice	*	*	*	*	*	*	*			*	*		*	*
Stock	*	*	*				*			*	*	*	*	*
Strawflower	*	*	*	*	*					*	*		*	*
Sunflower			*	*	*					*	*			*
Swan River Daisy	*	*				*	*			*	*		*	
Sweet Alyssum	*	*					*				*	*		
Sweet Pea	*	*	*			*	*				*	*	*	*
Sweet Potato Vine	*	*				*	*			*	*			*
Sweet William	*	*	*				*			*	*	*	*	*
Transvaal Daisy		*	*	*	*		*					*	*	
Verbena	*	*	*			*	*	*		*			*	*
Vinca Rosea	*	*	*							*			*	
Viola	*	*	*	*	*	*	*			*				
Wishbone Flower	*					*	*			*		*		
Zinnia	*	*	*	*	*		*	*		*	*	*	*	*

COLOR · SOWING · HEIGHT

Hardy	Half-hardy	Tender	Sun	Part Shade	Light Shade	Shade	Moist	Well Drained	Dry	Fertile	Average	Poor	Page Number	SPECIES by Common Name
*			*				*	*		*			206	Phlox
	*		*					*			*	*	208	Pincushion Flower
		*			*		*	*		*			210	Poor Man's Orchid
*			*					*		*			214	Poppy
*			*	*				*			*		218	Pot Marigold
	*		*					*			*	*	220	Prickly Poppy
*			*					*			*	*	222	Rock Cress
	*		*	*	*		*	*			*		224	Salvia
		*	*				*	*		*			228	Scarlet Runner Bean
*			*	*	*		*	*		*			230	Snapdragon
	*		*	*			*		*	*	*	*	234	Spider Flower
	*		*				*	*		*			238	Star Clusters
		*	*					*			*	*	240	Statice
*			*	*			*	*			*		242	Stock
		*	*				*	*	*		*		244	Strawflower
*			*				*	*			*		246	Sunflower
	*		*		*			*		*			250	Swan River Daisy
*			*		*		*	*			*	*	252	Sweet Alyssum
*			*		*		*	*		*			254	Sweet Pea
		*	*					*			*	*	258	Sweet Potato Vine
*			*		*			*			*		262	Sweet William
	*		*	*				*			*	*	266	Transvaal Daisy
		*	*					*	*	*	*		270	Verbena
		*	*	*			*		*	*	*	*	274	Vinca Rosea
*			*	*			*	*		*			276	Viola
		*	*	*			*			*			280	Wishbone Flower
		*	*				*	*		*			282	Zinnia

Glossary of Terms

acid soil: soil with a pH lower than 7.0

alkaline soil: soil with a pH higher than 7.0

annual: a plant that germinates, flowers, sets seed and dies in one growing season

basal leaves: leaves that form from the crown

biennial: a plant that germinates and produces stems, roots and leaves in the first growing season; it flowers, sets seed and dies in the second growing season

crown: the part of a plant at or just below soil level where the shoots join the roots

cultivar: a cultivated plant variety with one or more distinct differences from the species, such as flower color, leaf variegation or disease resistance

damping off: fungal disease causing seedlings to rot at soil level and topple over

deadhead: to remove spent flowers to maintain a neat appearance and encourage a longer blooming period

desiccation: drying out of plant tissue, especially foliage

disbud: to remove some flowerbuds to improve the size or quality of those remaining

dormancy: a period of plant inactivity, usually during winter or unfavorable climatic conditions

double flower: a flower with an unusually large number of petals, often caused by mutation of the stamens into petals

F1 hybrid: the first generation offspring of two closely related but distinct species or strains; usually more vigorous than the parent species and may have other desirable attributes. Self-pollination of F1 hybrids rarely produces plants that are true to type.

forma (f.): a naturally occurring variant of a species; below the level of subspecies in biological classification; similar to variety

genus: a category of biological classification between the species and family levels; the first word in a Latin name indicates the genus

half-hardy: a plant capable of surviving the climatic conditions of a given region if protected

harden off: to gradually acclimatize plants that have been growing in a protective environment to a more harsh environment, e.g., plants started indoors being moved outdoors

hardy: capable of surviving unfavorable conditions, such as cold weather

humus: decomposed or decomposing organic material in the soil

hybrid: a plant resulting from natural or human-induced crossbreeding between varieties, species, or genera; the hybrid expresses features of each parent plant

neutral soil: soil with a pH of 7.0

node: the area on a stem from which a leaf or new shoot grows

pH: a measure of acidity or alkalinity (the lower the pH, the higher the acidity); the pH of soil influences availability of nutrients for plants

perennial: a plant that takes three or more years to complete its life cycle; a herbaceous perennial normally dies back to the ground over winter

quilled: refers to the narrow, tubular shape of petals or florets of certain flowers

rhizome: a food-storing stem that grows horizontally at or just below soil level, from which new shoots may emerge

rootball: the root mass and surrounding soil of a container-grown plant or a plant dug out of the ground

runner: a modified stem that grows on the soil surface; roots and new shoots are produced at nodes along its length

semi-double flower: a flower with petals that form two or three rings

side-dressing: applying fertilizer to the soil beside or around a plant during the growing season to stimulate growth

single flower: a flower with a single ring of typically four or five petals

species: the original species from which cultivars and varieties are derived; the fundamental unit of biological classification

subspecies (subsp.): a naturally occurring, regional form of a species, often isolated from other subspecies but still potentially interfertile with them

taproot: a root system consisting of one main root with smaller roots branching from it

tender: incapable of surviving the climatic conditions of a given region and requiring protection from frost or cold

tepal: a sepal or petal of a flower, when the petals and sepals are not clearly distinguished from each other

true: the passing of desirable characteristics from the parent plant to seed-grown offspring; also called breeding true to type

tuber: the thick section of a rhizome bearing nodes and buds

variegation: foliage that has more than one color, often patched or striped or bearing differently colored leaf margins

variety (var.): a naturally occurring variant of a species; below the level of subspecies in biological classification

Glossary of Pests & Diseases

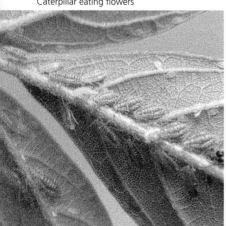

Caterpillar eating flowers

Aphids (center), Ladybird beetle larva (below)

Anthracnose

Fungus. Yellow or brown spots on leaves; sunken lesions and blisters on stems; can kill plant.
What to Do. Choose resistant varieties and cultivars; keep soil well drained; thin out stems to improve air circulation; avoid handling wet foliage. Remove and destroy infected plant parts; clean up and destroy debris from infected plants at end of growing season. Liquid copper spray can prevent the spread of the disease to other susceptible plants.

Aphids

Tiny, pear-shaped insects, winged or wingless; green, black, brown, red or gray. Cluster along stems, on buds and on leaves. Suck sap from plants; cause distorted or stunted growth. Sticky honeydew forms on surfaces and encourages sooty mold growth.
What to Do. Squish small colonies by hand; dislodge them with water spray; spray serious infestations with insecticidal soap or horticultural oil; many predatory insects and birds feed on them.

Beetles

Many types and sizes; usually rounded in shape with hard, shell-like outer wings covering membranous inner wings. Some are beneficial, e.g., ladybird beetles ('ladybugs'); others, e.g., June beetles, eat plants. Larvae: see Borers, Grubs. Leave wide range of chewing damage: make small or large holes in or around margins of leaves; consume entire leaves or areas between leaf veins ('skeletonize'); may also chew holes in flowers.
What to Do. Pick beetles off at night and drop them into an old coffee can half filled with soapy water (soap prevents them from floating); spread an old sheet under plants and shake off beetles

to collect and dispose of them. Use a hand-held vacuum cleaner to remove them from the plant. Beneficial nematodes are effective control if the beetle goes through a part of its growing cycle in the ground.

Borers

Larvae of some moths, wasps, beetles; among the most damaging plant pests. Burrow into plant stems, branches, leaves and/or roots; destroy vascular tissue (plant veins and arteries) and structural strength. Worm-like; vary in size and get bigger as they bore through plants. Burrow and weaken stems to cause breakage; leaves will wilt; may see tunnels in leaves, stems or roots; rhizomes may be hollowed out entirely or in part.

What to Do. May be able to squish borers within leaves. Remove and destroy bored parts; may need to dig up and destroy infected roots and rhizomes.

Lygos bug on cosmos

Budworms (Geranium Budworm, Tobacco Budworm)

Moth larvae. $1/2$ to $3/4$" long; striped; green, yellow-green, tan, dull red; bore into buds, eat from inside out and sometimes on open flowers; also eat new leaf growth; buds and new leaves appear tattered or ridden with holes.

What to Do. Pick off by hand daily and drop in soapy water. Remove infested plants and destroy. Preventative spray of B.t. *(Bacillus thuringiensis)* on mature plants. Don't re-plant susceptible varieties.

Bugs (True Bugs)

Small insects, up to $1/2$" long; green, brown, black or brightly colored and patterned. Many beneficial; a few pierce plants to suck out sap. Toxins may be injected that deform plants; sunken areas left where pierced; leaves rip as they grow; leaves, buds and new growth may be dwarfed and deformed.

What to Do. Remove debris and weeds from around plants in fall to destroy overwintering sites. Pick off by hand and drop into soapy water. Use parasitic nematodes if part of the bug's growth cycle is in the ground.

Caterpillars

Larvae of butterflies, moths, sawflies. Include budworms (see Budworms), cutworms (see Cutworms), leaf rollers, leaf tiers, loopers. Chew foliage and buds. Can completely defoliate a plant if infestation severe.

What to Do. Removal from plant is best control. Use high-pressure water and soap, or pick caterpillars off by hand. Control biologically using the naturally occurring soil bacterium *Bacillus thuringiensis* var. *kurstaki*, or B.t. for short (commercially available), which breaks down gut lining of caterpillars.

Cutworms

Larvae of some moths. About 1" long; plump, smooth-skinned caterpillars; curl up when poked or disturbed. Usually affect only young plants and seedlings, which may be completely chewed off at ground level.

What to Do. Pick off by hand. Create physical barriers from old toilet tissue

rolls to make collars around plant bases; push tubes at least halfway into ground. Another trick is to put three toothpicks around each plant; make sure the toothpicks are right up against the stem.

Gray Mold (Botrytis Blight)

Fungal disease. Leaves, stems and flowers blacken, rot and die.

What to Do. Thin stems to improve air circulation, keep mulch away from base of plant, particularly in spring when plant starts to sprout; remove debris from garden at end of growing season; do not overwater. Remove and destroy any infected plant parts. Use horticultural oil as a preventative measure. Compost tea is also effective.

Grubs

Larvae of different beetles, commonly found below soil level; usually curled in C-shape. Body white or gray; head may be white, gray, brown or reddish. Problematic in lawns; may feed on plant roots. Plant wilts despite regular watering; may pull easily out of ground in severe cases.

What to Do. Toss any grubs found while digging onto a stone path or patio for birds to devour; apply parasitic nematodes or milky disease spore to infested soil (ask at your local garden center).

Moth on strawflower (above),
Leaf miner damage (below)

Leaf Miners

Tiny, stubby larvae of some butterflies and moths; may be yellow or green. Tunnel within leaves leaving winding trails; tunneled areas lighter in color than rest of leaf. Unsightly rather than health risk to plant.

What to Do. Remove debris from area in fall to destroy overwintering sites; attract parasitic wasps with nectar plants such as yarrows. Remove and destroy infected foliage; can sometimes squish by hand within leaf. Floating row covers prevent eggs from being laid on plant. Bright blue sticky cards, available in most nurseries and through mail order, will attract and trap adult leaf miners.

Leaf Spot

Two common types: one caused by bacteria and the other by fungi. *Bacterial*: small speckled spots grow to encompass entire leaves; brown or purple in color; leaves may drop. *Fungal*: black, brown or yellow spots; leaves wither.
What to Do. Bacterial infection more severe; must remove entire plant. For fungal infection, remove and destroy infected plant parts. Sterilize removal tools; avoid wetting foliage or touching wet foliage; remove and destroy debris at end of growing season. Spray plant with liquid copper. Compost tea also works in most instances.

Mealybugs

Tiny crawling insects related to aphids; appear to be covered with white fuzz or flour. Sucking damage stunts and stresses plant. Mealybugs excrete honeydew, which promotes growth of sooty mold.
What to Do. Remove by hand on smaller plants; wash plant off with soap and water; wipe off with alcohol-soaked swabs; remove leaves with heavy infestations; encourage or introduce natural predators such as mealybug destroyer beetle and parasitic wasps; spray with insecticidal soap. Keep in mind larvae of mealybug destroyer beetles look like very large mealybugs. Always check plants for mealybugs before buying.

Mildew

Two types, both caused by fungus, but with slightly different symptoms. *Downy mildew:* yellow spots on upper sides of leaves and downy fuzz on undersides; fuzz may be yellow, white or gray. *Powdery mildew:* white or gray powdery coating on leaf surfaces that doesn't brush off.
What to Do. Choose resistant cultivars; space plants well; thin stems to encourage air circulation; tidy any debris in fall. Remove and destroy infected leaves or other parts. Spray compost tea or highly diluted fish emulsion (1 teaspoon per quart of water) to control powdery mildew. Control downy mildew by spraying foliage with a mixture of 5 tablespoons of horticultural oil and 2 teaspoons of baking soda per gallon of water. Three applications at one-week intervals will be needed.

Nematodes

Tiny worms that give plants disease symptoms. One type infects foliage and stems; the other infects roots. *Foliar:* yellow spots that turn brown on leaves; leaves shrivel and wither; problem starts on lowest leaves and works up plant. *Root-knot:* plant is stunted; may wilt; yellow spots on leaves; roots have tiny bumps or knots.
What to Do. Mulch soil, add organic matter, clean up debris in fall. Don't touch wet foliage of infected plants; can add parasitic nematodes to soil. Remove infected plants in extreme cases.

Psyllids

Tiny, gnat-like insects that suck juice out of plant leaves, causing foliage to yellow, curl and die or appear brown and blasted; may leave sticky honeydew on leaves, encouraging sooty mold growth. Adults are $1/10$" long, green or brown and have wings; young nymphs have a white, waxy coating and are nearly immobile.

Powdery mildew on zinnia

Snail eating leaf

What to Do. Remove and destroy infested plants; do not put infested plants in compost bin. Keep area free of weeds. Ensure good fall clean up. Diatomaceous earth (not the kind used for swimming pools) or sulfur dusted on foliage may kill nymphs.

Rot

Several different fungi that affect different parts of the plant and can kill plant. *Crown rot:* affects base of plant, causing stems to blacken and fall over and leaves to yellow and wilt. *Root rot:* leaves yellow and plant wilts; digging up plant will show roots rotted away.
What to Do. Keep soil well drained; don't damage plant if you are digging around it; keep mulches away from plant base. Remove any infected plants.

Rust

Fungi. Pale spots on upper leaf surfaces; orange, fuzzy or dusty spots on leaf undersides.
What to Do. Choose rust-resistant varieties and cultivars; avoid handling wet leaves; provide plant with good air circulation; use horticultural oil to protect new foliage; clean up garden debris at end of season. Remove and destroy infected plant parts. Do not put infected plants in compost pile.

Slugs & Snails

Slugs lack shells; snails have a spiral shell; both have slimy, smooth skin; can be up to 8" long; gray, green, black, beige, yellow or spotted. Leave large ragged hole in leaves and silvery slime trails on and around plants.
What to Do. Attach strips of copper to wood around raised beds or smaller boards inserted around susceptible groups of plants; slugs and snails will get shocked if they touch copper surfaces. Pick off by hand in the evening and squish with boot or drop in can of soapy water. Spread wood ash, oyster shells or diatomaceous earth (available in garden centers) on ground around plants; it will pierce their soft bodies and cause them to dehydrate. CAUTION: do not use the diatomoaceous earth that is used for swimming pool filters. Use slug and snail bait, also available at local garden centers. Beer in a shallow dish may be effective.

Smut

Fungus. Attacks any above-ground plant parts including leaves, stems and flowers. Forms fleshy white galls that turn black and powdery.
What to Do. Remove and destroy infected plants. Avoid planting same plants in that spot for next few years.

Sooty Mold

Fungus. Thin black film forms on leaf surfaces and reduces amount of light getting to leaf surfaces.
What to Do. Wipe mold off leaf surfaces; control insects such as aphids, mealybugs, whiteflies (honeydew left on leaves encourages mold).

Spider Mites

Almost invisible to the naked eye; relatives of spiders without their insect-eating habits. Tiny; eight-legged; may spin webs; red, yellow or green; usually found on undersides of plant leaves. Suck juice out of leaves; may see fine webbing on leaves and stems; may see mites moving on leaf undersides; leaves become

discolored and speckled in appearance, then turn brown and shrivel up.
What to Do: Wash off with a strong spray of water daily until all signs of infestation are gone; predatory mites are available through garden centers; spray plants with insecticidal soap. Apply horticultural oil.

Thrips

Difficult to see; may be visible if you disturb them by blowing gently on an infested flower. Yellow, black or brown; tiny, slender; narrow fringed wings. Suck juice out of plant cells, particularly in flowers and buds, causing gray mottled petals and leaves, dying buds and distorted and stunted growth.
What to Do. Remove and destroy infected plant parts; encourage native predatory insects with nectar plants such as yarrows; spray severe infestations with insecticidal soap. Use horticultural oil at 5 tablespoons per gallon. Use sticky blue cards to attract and trap adults.

Viruses

Plant may be stunted and leaves and flowers distorted, streaked or discolored. Viral diseases in plants cannot be controlled.
What to Do: Destroy infected plants; control insects such as aphids, leafhoppers and whiteflies that spread disease.

Whiteflies

Tiny flying insects that flutter up into the air when the plant is disturbed. Tiny; moth-like; white; live on undersides of plant leaves. Suck juice out of plant leaves, causing yellowed leaves and weakened plants; leave sticky honeydew on leaves, encouraging sooty mold growth.
What to Do. Destroy weeds where insects may live. Attract native predatory beetles and parasitic wasps with nectar plants such as yarrows; spray severe cases with insecticidal soap. Can make a sticky flypaper-like trap by mounting tin can on stake; wrap can

Ladybird beetles are beneficial garden predators.

with yellow paper and cover with clear baggie smeared with petroleum jelly; replace baggie when full of flies. Yellow sticky cards are also available from local nurseries and garden centers. Plant Sweet Alyssum in the immediate area. Make a spray by boiling old coffee grounds (see recipe p. 147) and use liquid as a spray.

Wilt

If watering hasn't helped a wilted plant, one of two wilt fungi may be at fault. *Fusarium wilt:* plant wilts, leaves turn yellow then die; symptoms generally appear first on one part of plant before spreading to other parts. *Verticillium wilt:* plant wilts; leaves curl up at edges; leaves turn yellow then drop off; plant may die.
What to Do. Both wilts difficult to control. Choose resistant plant varieties and cultivars; clean up debris at end of growing season. Destroy infected plants; solarize (sterilize) soil before re-planting—contact local garden center for assistance.

Index

Page numbers in **bold** indicate main flower headings.